Fantasies
Wide Awake

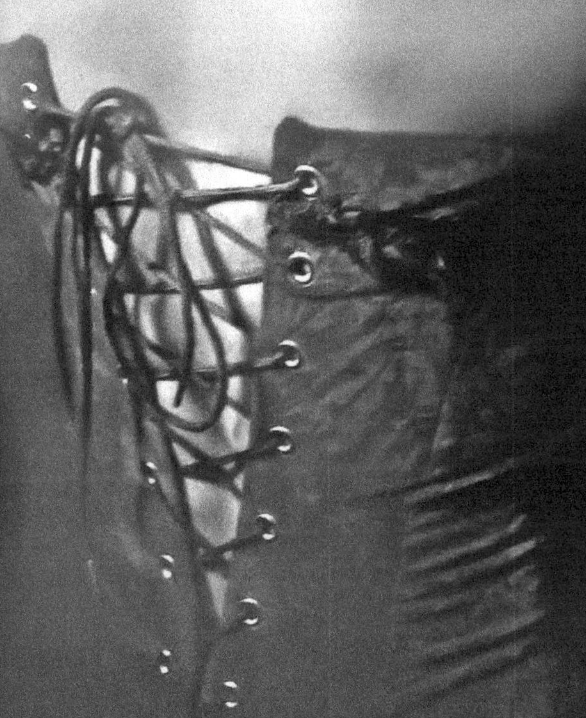

LaShawnda Jones

Harvest Books
Second Edition

Printed on-demand regionally by IngramSpark. LaShawnda Jones's books may be purchased in bulk for promotional, educational, or business use. Please contact your local bookseller or email LaShawnda Jones, Harvest Books at Shawnda@Harvest-Life.org.

Cover photo by Shalina Ali.
Project photography by Lisa Richelle.
Additional credits in back of book.

SECOND EDITION

Library of Congress Control Number: 2005903878
Print ISBN 10: 0-9776179-6-3
Print ISBN 13: 978-0-9776179-6-8
eBook ISBN 13: 978-0-9776179-1-3

This volume is dedicated to the muses from my young adult years. Thank you all for enriching my imagination simply by being yourselves.

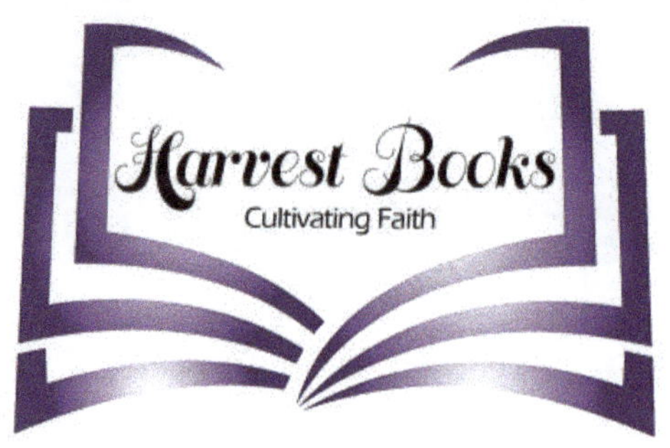

Books by LaShawnda Jones

I AM WOMAN: Expressions of Black Womanhood in America
Desert of Solitude: Refreshed by Grace
My God and Me: Listening, Learning and Growing on My Journey
The Process of Asking for, Receiving & Giving Love & Forgiveness
Clichés: A Life in Verse
Fantasies: Wide Awake

Contributor
Go, Tell Michelle: African American Women Write to the New First Lady

Available on
Amazon
BN.com
Harvest-Life.org/shop

Connect on Social Media

Blog: Harvest-Life.org/blog
@HarvestLifer
on Anchor, Fanbase, Instagram, Opensea, Patreon, Twitter

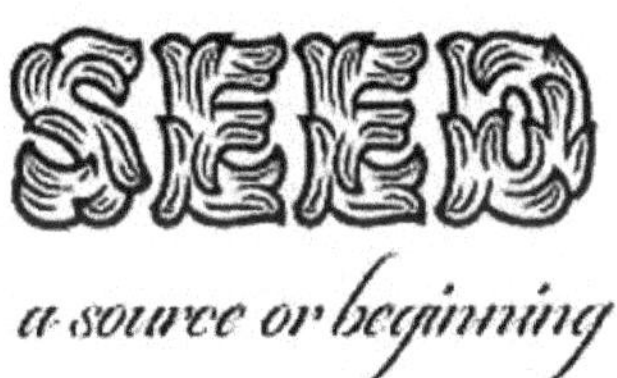

a source or beginning

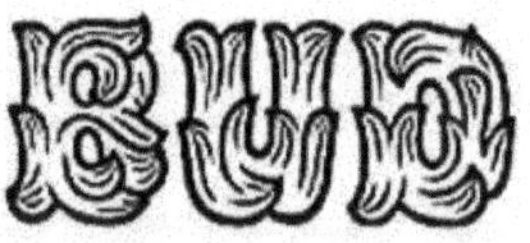

a person or thing that is not yet fully developed
to be in an undeveloped stage or condition

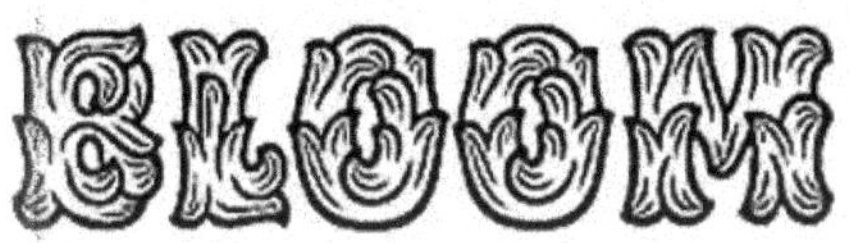

The condition of being in flower.
a condition or time of vigor and beauty.
Prime.

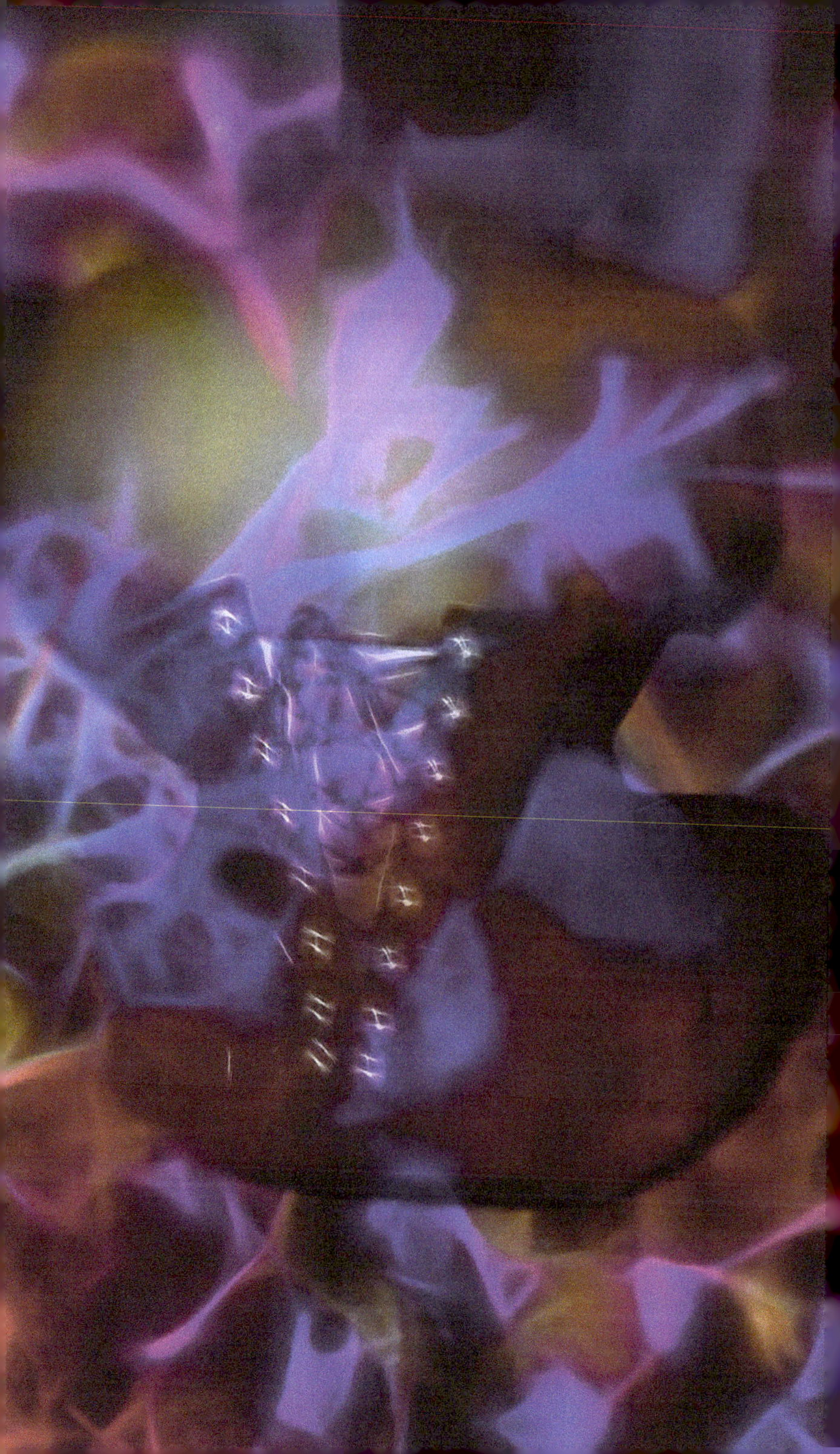

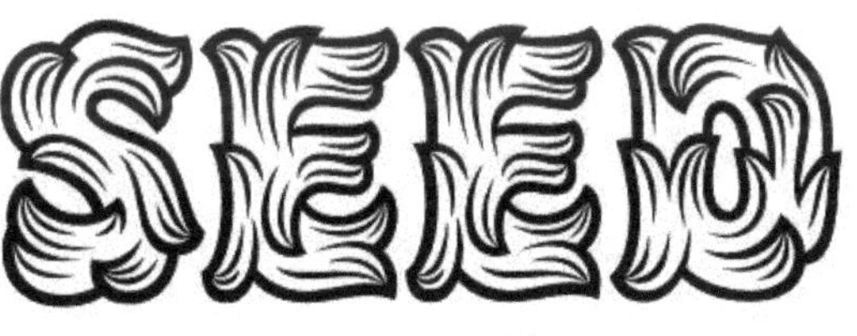

a source or beginning

The New Eve

The new Eve is not a
virginal woman
but a woman
who lacks experience.
She's a woman who
offers a different kind
of temptation to the same Adam

Sometimes, I think
I am a new Eve –
Not virgin, but without
temptation to offer anyone.
I'm just inexperienced.
Living without love.
Without a lover.

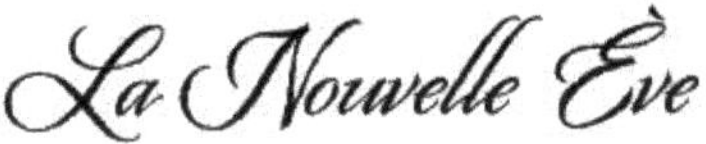

La nouvelle Ève est une femme
qui n'est pas une vierge
mais une femme
sans expérience.
Elle est une femme
Qui offre un autre type
De tentation au meme Adam.

Quelquefois je pense que
Je suis une nouvelle Ève
Pas vierge mais sans de
Tentation offrir personne
Je suis juste inexperimentée.
Vivre sans amour.
Sans un amant .

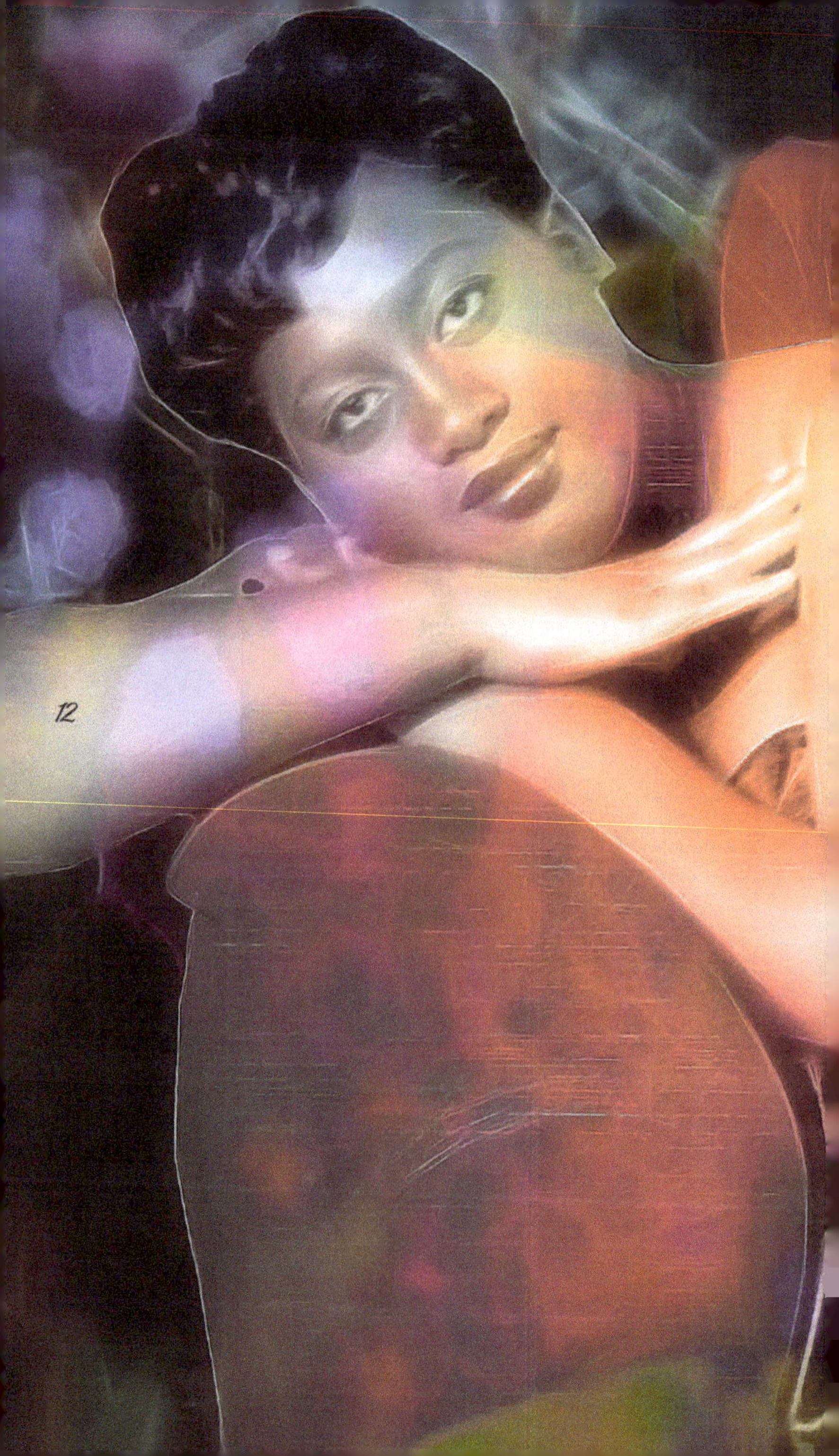

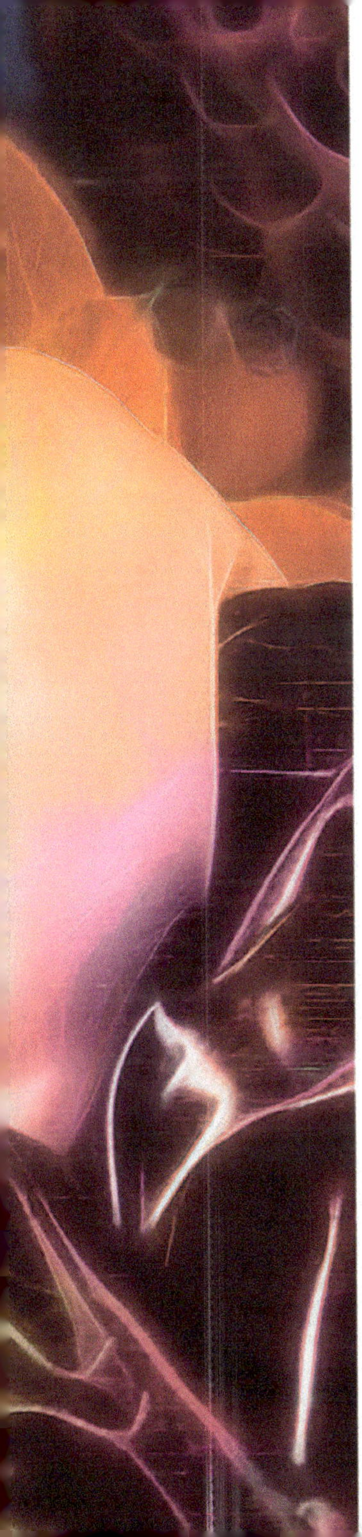

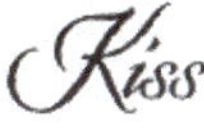

To touch your lips
In a gentle caress
To touch mine to
Your sculptured chest
To shape your lips with
My tongue as you rest
To feel your lips nip
And suckle my breasts
So many ways have I
Longed for your kiss

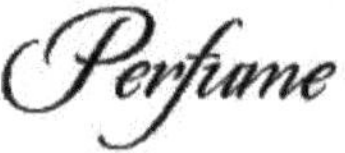

Perfume
Accentuates my sensuousness
Urging me to
Rejoice in my voluptuousness
Exploit my sexiness while
Stimulating my desires

Perfume
Blankets me in sweet invitation
Causing me to
Gesticulate in his direction
Imitating age-old woman's machinations
Acting on my dreams

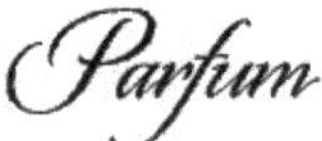

Parfum
Qui accentue ma sensualité
M'incite
À me réjouir dans ma volupté,
À exploiter mes charmes
Tout en stimulant mes désirs

Parfum
Qui me baigne d'une douce invitation,
Me faisant
Gesticuler vers lui
Imitant les intrigues féminines de toujours
Inspirant mes rêves

The Number - 1

Yesterday I felt joy
I floated on clouds of hope
anxious for this dawn
to transform
into dusk
so I could call

The Number - 2

Fluttery anticipation
eager imagination
tall handsome young
jock specimen
has me all atwitter
convulsing in giggles
overheating in flashes

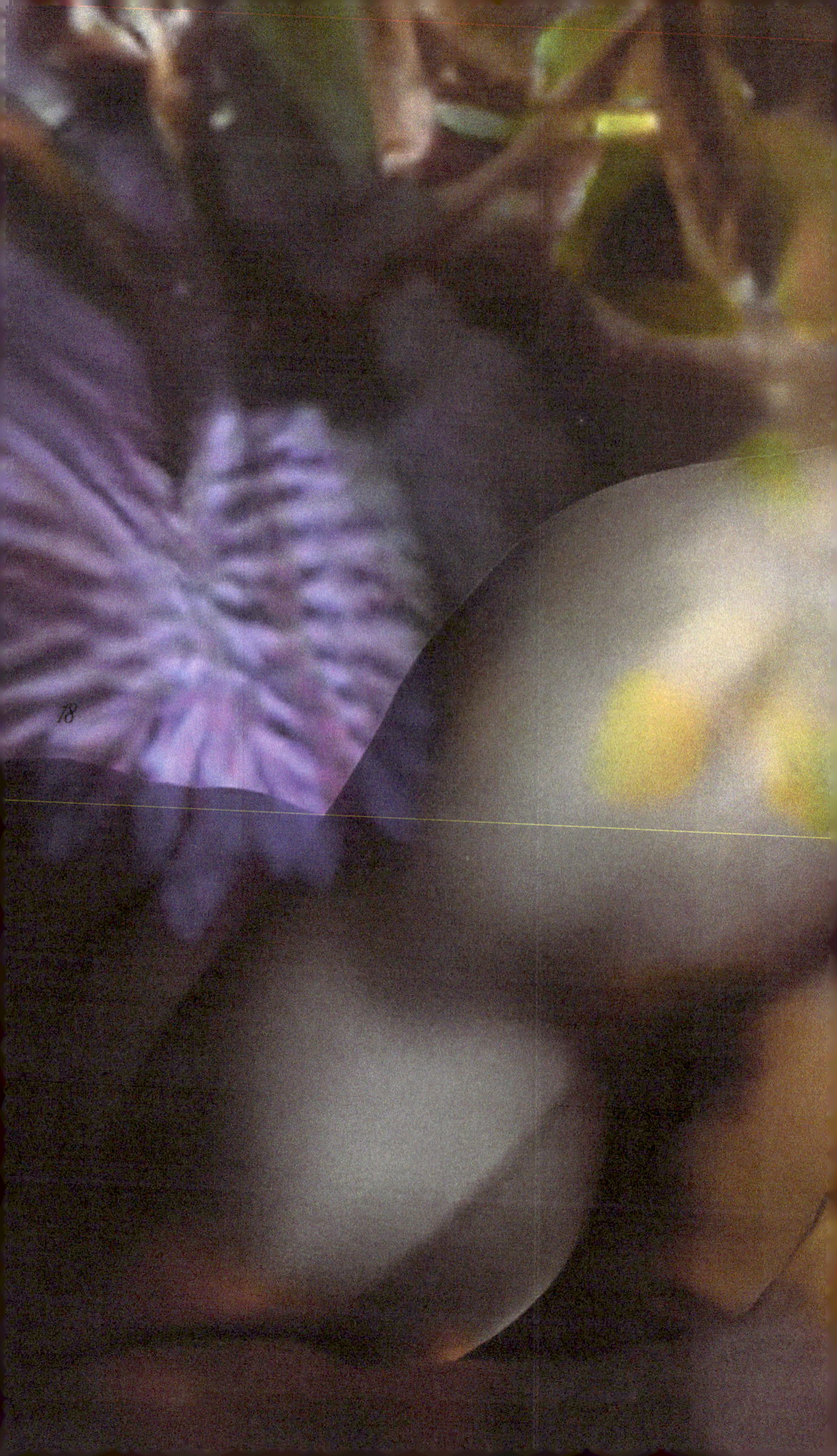

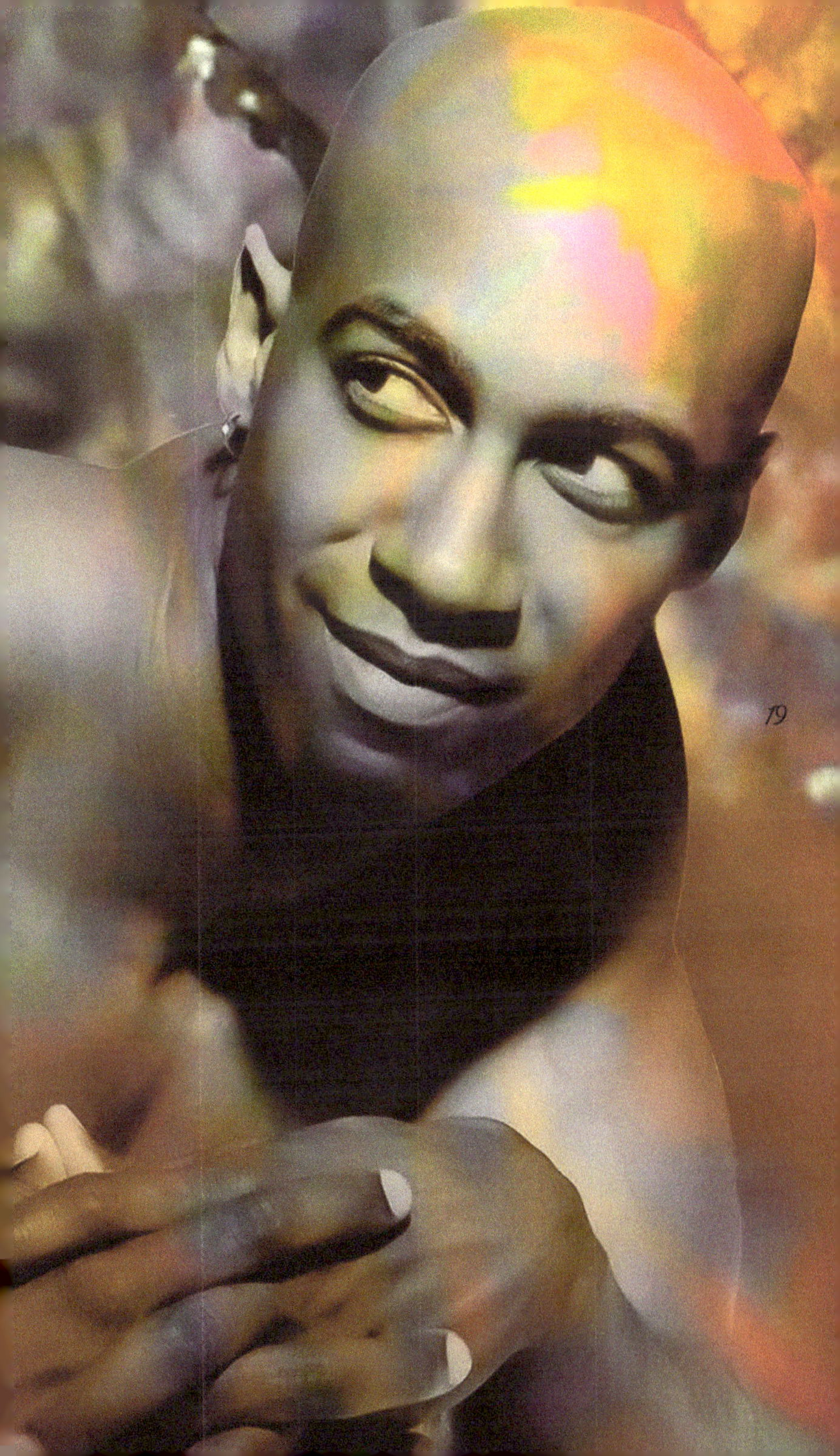

The Number - 3

Age is more than
a number

Age is experience
a little more direction,
sometimes maturity,
a drop of
understanding patience
or is that
patient understanding?

Age is a journey
to knowing and
accepting yourself;
learning, loving, and
improving yourself

Age is so much more
than the passage of time.
It's a way of marking progress,
structuring goals,
and developing
your being.

Damn, Baby!

Damn!
I wish I was your lover.
Damn! I wish you were inside me,
On me, caressing me.
I wish our tongues could meet and dual,
Parry and retreat.
Teeth nipping and nibbling
Lips seeking and contouring
As our breath merge.
Damn, I wish I was your lover!

Hell!
I wish you were mine.
Hell, I wish I had the right
To climb all over you,
Push up against you, be part of you.
I want to know the texture of your skin
From your forehead to the bottom of your feet.
As my lips detail the contours of your body.
Hell, I wish you were mine!

Baby!
I wish we were together.
Baby, I wish I could grab your hands
And cup them to my throbbing breasts.
Hold your mouth at my throat,
As your hips take control, rocking to
A rhythm of their own – long, smooth and hard;
I cling to you, as you take me home.
Oh, baby, I wish we were together..

Tariq II

Few are like me…
Leastways, I can't find one near
Equal in needs....

Few hunger like me...
And I know no other on the prowl like me.

Searching....
Have you ever felt a lack so deeply,
That seeing a glimmer of possibility
Of that something in someone
Makes your heart soar; your soul sigh.
And you know contentment,
A bliss of anticipation?

I do.
I lack.
I saw.

Hope needs only a glimmer,
A smidgen of possibility
And new life takes shape in the mind.

Shared.

No longer empty.
A smidgen and suddenly
I scrape the edge of understanding
That male-female connection
My mind races ahead to experience

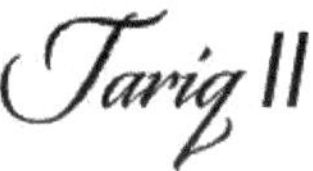

Peu sont comme moi
Du moins, je n'en trouve pas un
près de m'égaler en besoins…

Peu ont faim comme moi…
Personne que je connaisse rôdant comme moi.

Cherchant.....
Que vous a-t-il déjà manqué si profondement,
Que voir une lueur de possibilité
De ce quelque chose en quelqu'un
Votre coeur s'envole, votre âme soupire.
À vous le contentement,
Une volupté d'anticipation.

Je fais.
Je manque.
Je voyais.

L'espoir se suffit d'une lueur
D'un rien de potentiel
Et la vie se dessine dans l'esprit.

Partagée.

N'est plus vide.
Un brin et soudain
Je gratte le bord de la compréhension
Cette connexion homme-femme
Mon esprit s'emballe pour expérimenter

All that could fill the void,
starting with a
A companion and friend.

I fantasized based on an illusion.
That smidgen
Inspired by imperfection.
Inspired by man.
The fantasy dissipated
When the glimmer passed.

Tout ce qui pourrait combler le vide,
en commençant par un
Un compagnon et un ami.

J'ai fantasmé sur la base d'une illusion.
Ce brin
Inspiré par l'imperfection.
Inspiré par l'homme.
Le fantasme s'est dissipé
Quand la lueur est passée

Sexual Tension

My blood is molten,
My heart runs rapid,
My breath quickens.

Another heart beat.
I throb -
My breasts peak.
In my bed, I lie
With my eyes closed,
I sigh.

My toes curl,
My limbs become heavy,
In my belly, a butterfly unfurls.

Relaxing is hard to do
When my mind won't
Clear away remnants of you.

Two Smiles

Smiling lips
are ordinary
commonplace
a simple grace

A smiling body
quite an extra-
ordinary starburst
in which to rejoice

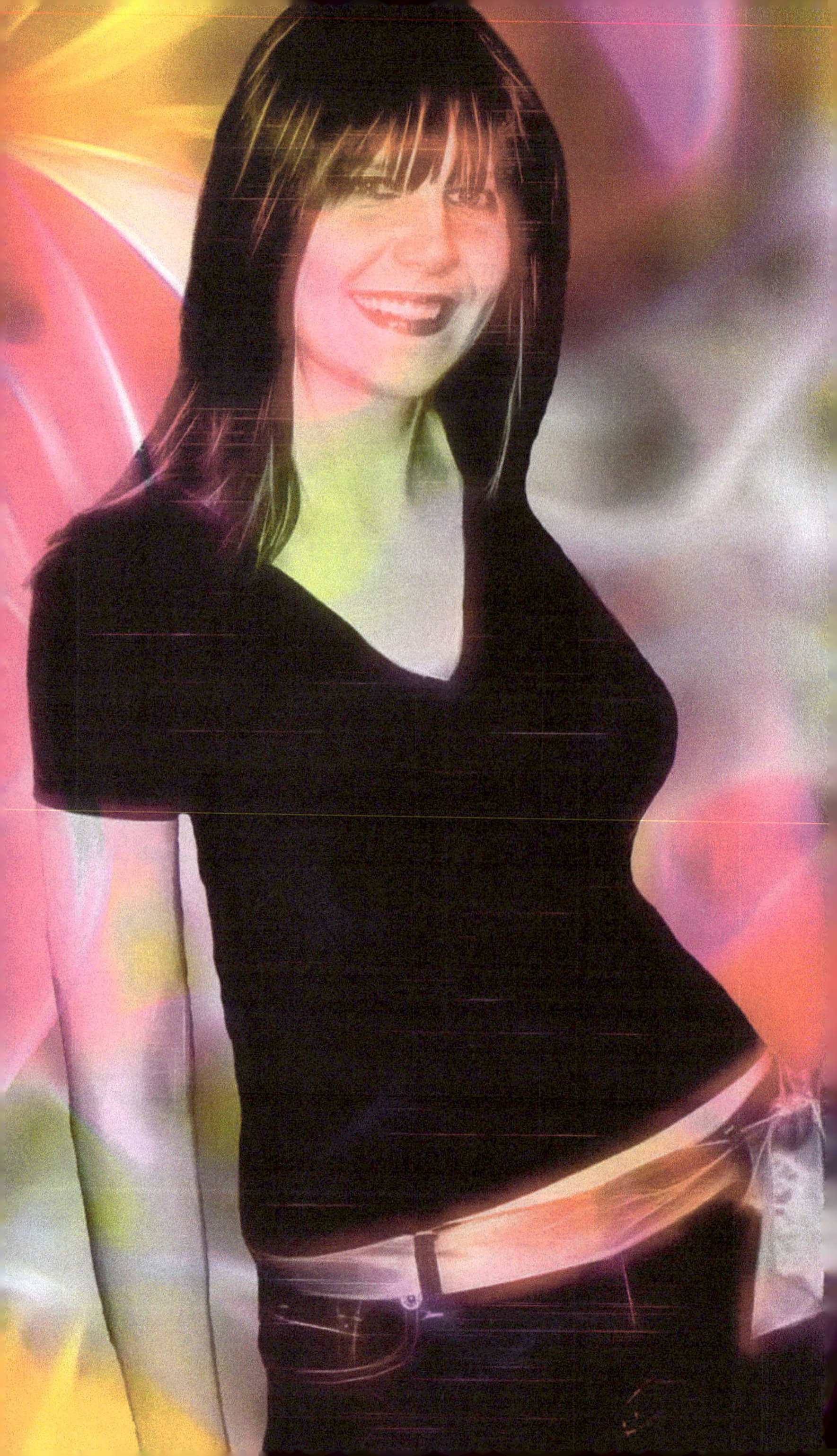

The One and The Other

The One is here
The Other is not.
Just missed him.
Am I happy?
Sad? Do I care?
It's hard to tell.
My heartbeat
doubles at the mention
of the One,
always eager
for his presence.

And the Other?
It's okay he's not here
my pulse needs a rest.
He's so sexy….
between the two
I stay breathless
and euphoric.

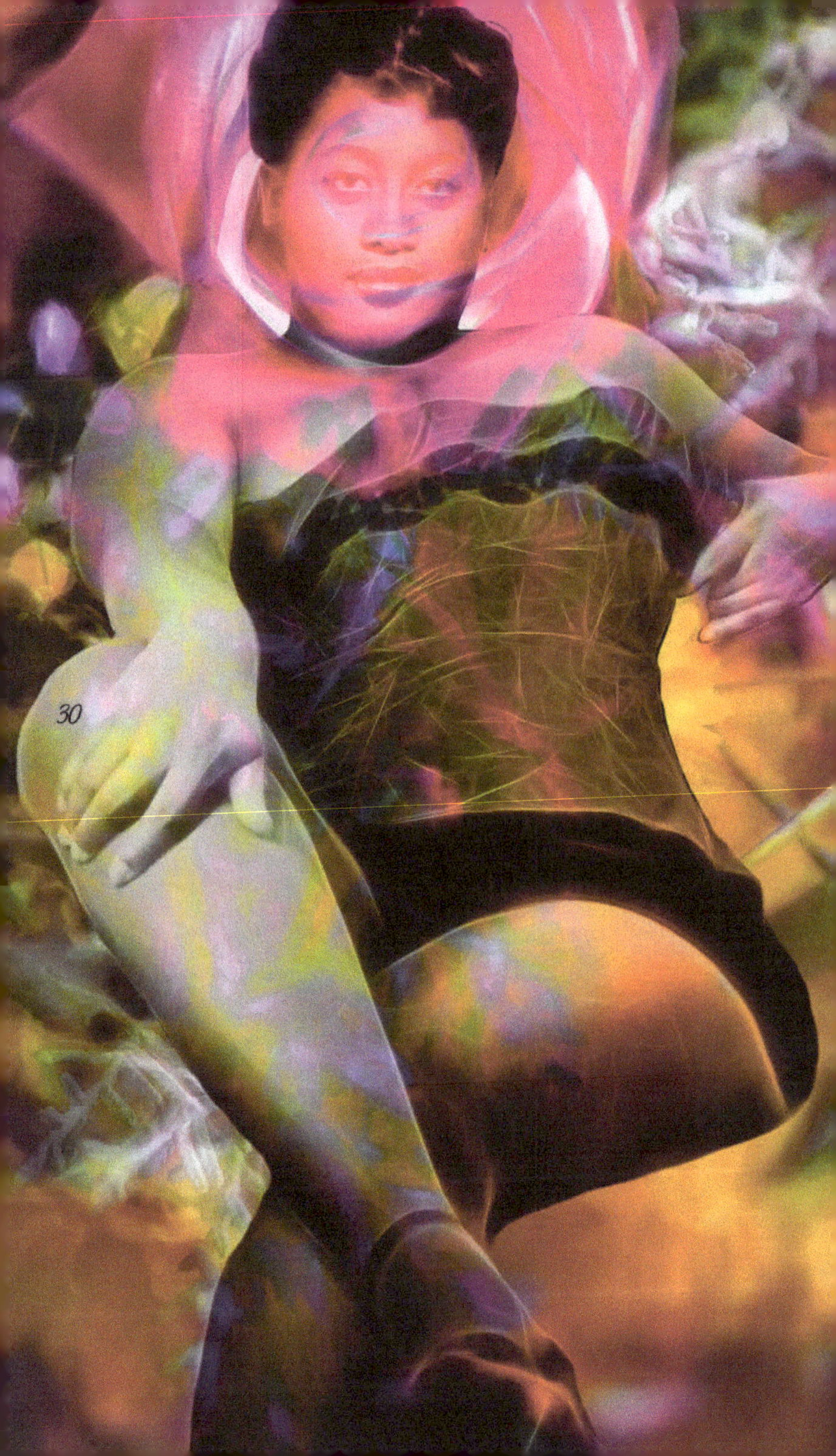

Beauty, Laughter, Love, Joy in Life

Beauty...
Beauty is in the eye of the beholder
I've been gazed upon, but never held
It's a moment I'd love to sway in,
Blush in,
Preen in.

Laughter...
Laughter is a life-giving sound
I've never shared with a love
A sound I imagine caressing my neck
in puffs of air
and searching lips.

Love...
Love is mutual existence
A way of life foreign to me
An existence I crave
for substance
and purpose.

Joy...
Joy is sustenance
A nourishing requirement for healthy life
Strengthening mind and spirit
rewarding survivors
allowing thrivers to rejoice.

And life...
My life is a stage
In need of a leading man
A stage we could both
Shine on
Dance on
Rejoice on,
Be beautiful on.

Thinking Out Loud

Okay, baby,
I admit you got me.
I'm stuck, I'm whipped
and you've put nothing
on me but your
intense gaze.
I've seen your smiles
your smug smirks
as you scored points
by getting one over on me.
Perhaps it was the way
you flexed your arms,
the way you stretched
your calves, or perhaps
it was the sexy swagger
you utilized to walk past me.
So intentionally prancing
your glorious body past me.
Are you really so adept
at reading my body language?
Are you truly aware
of the effect you, your smile,
your movements have on me?
Have you witnessed the
dreamy closing of my lids
as I forced my eyes to
roll away from you?
Have you noticed my
deepening breaths play havoc
with the thrust of my breasts?
Are you aware of my
inability to lift weights

when your eyes perform
their sensual assault?
Do you see the quivers ripple across my
body?
You may say ***no***, but your
grin says ***yes***.
So, okay, baby,
I admit you got me.
But, I don't mind being whipped,
if you're in the same state I'm in.
Admit it.
I got you
too, don't I, baby?

I'm reading your body language,

observing your habits and
noting your adjustments.
Am I affecting
you so strongly?
You may say no, but your
stiffness says yes.
It's okay, baby.
I don't want to hurt you.
Just want to love you
and love you
and love you some more.

Your prancing is nerve-racking
but I adore your confident swagger.

The intensity of your gaze
on me scares me, even as I hunger
for your presence. But I'm able

to give back some of my
own here and there. I know
you like my derrière, especially
in the tight red bikers.
My hips swing in a wider
arch for you on those biker nights.
The curve of my back is more
pronounced. My walk mimics
your swagger then.
You like that, don't you, baby?
Those nights you always try
to get close to me – standing
right behind me, occupying
the machine next to me.
Close, but not close enough.
And all too soon,
quite abruptly, you leave
in the middle of a set,
well before your normal time.
The abrupt clanging
of your dropped weights are a
shock to my system but
a balm to my ego.
What, you couldn't handle it?
Scared you can't handle me?
Do you see my satisfied
smirks as I mentally mark
the board in my favor?

Do you want me or are
you just teasing me?

All this time, my attraction
has not waned, it has
remained constant.
Your eyes have not strayed
from me either. So why don't
you admit it? Why don't you
follow through with what
you truly want?
You want me.
Go ahead, snatch me up;
I promise not to resist.

Awakening

I can't let it flow
I can't seem to let go
of myself, of my feelings
I can't love blindly
I can't sex casually
with him, with anyone
I can't walk in faith
I can't put value on what's said
by this man, my awakener
I want to relax myself
uncover my sexual wealth
I want to love without reservation
but there's too much to think about
to my consternation
I want to trust in his experience
but too much doesn't speak of success,
hence,
my hesitation
with his flirtation
continuing to an irrevocable end

I'd rather keep it simple and not bend
I'd rather remain aloof

You keep your cool
for I won't let my emotions flow
I won't let myself go
I won't love you blindly
I won't sex you casually
but thanks for awakening me
I now recognize my sexual beauty

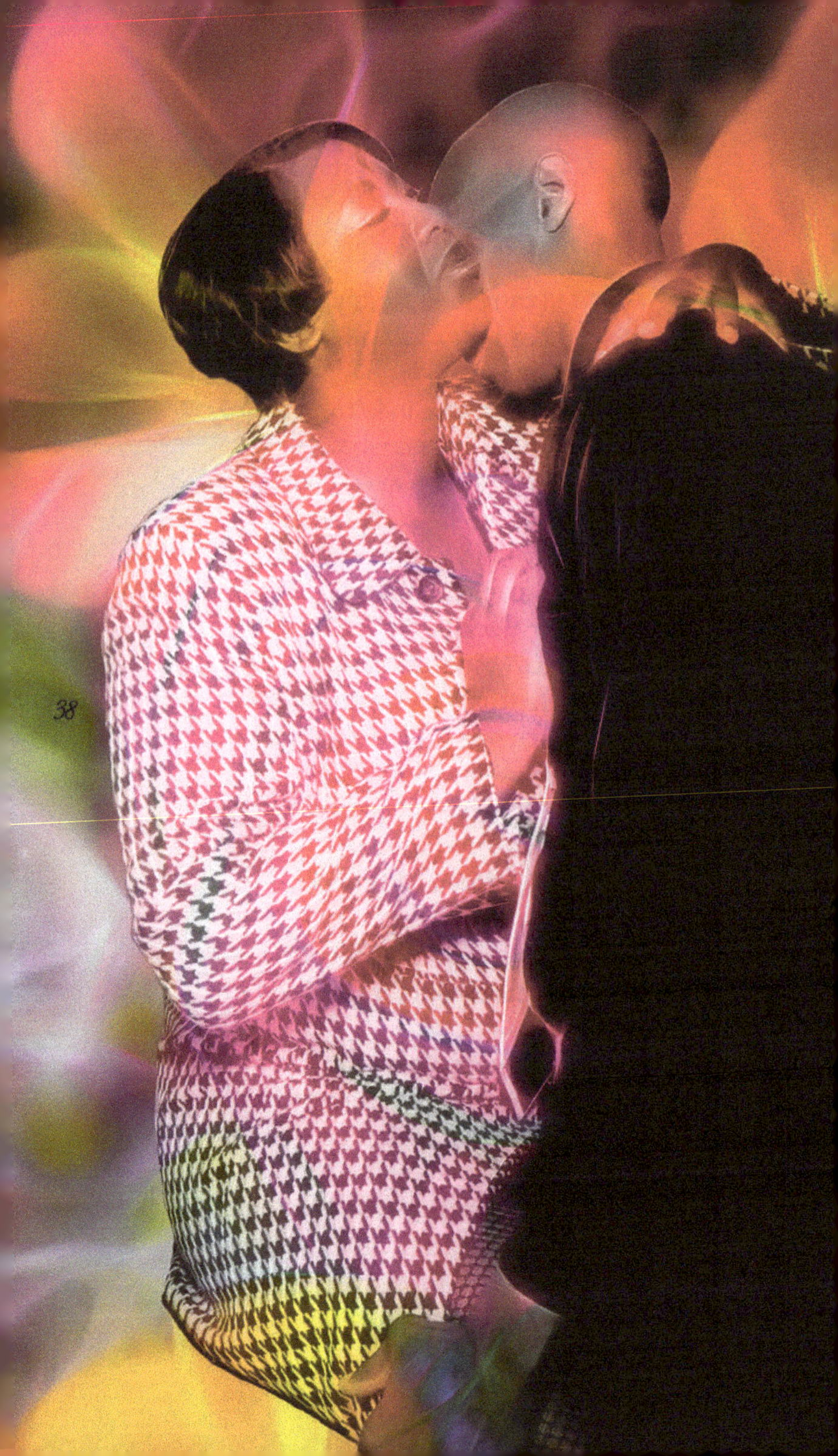

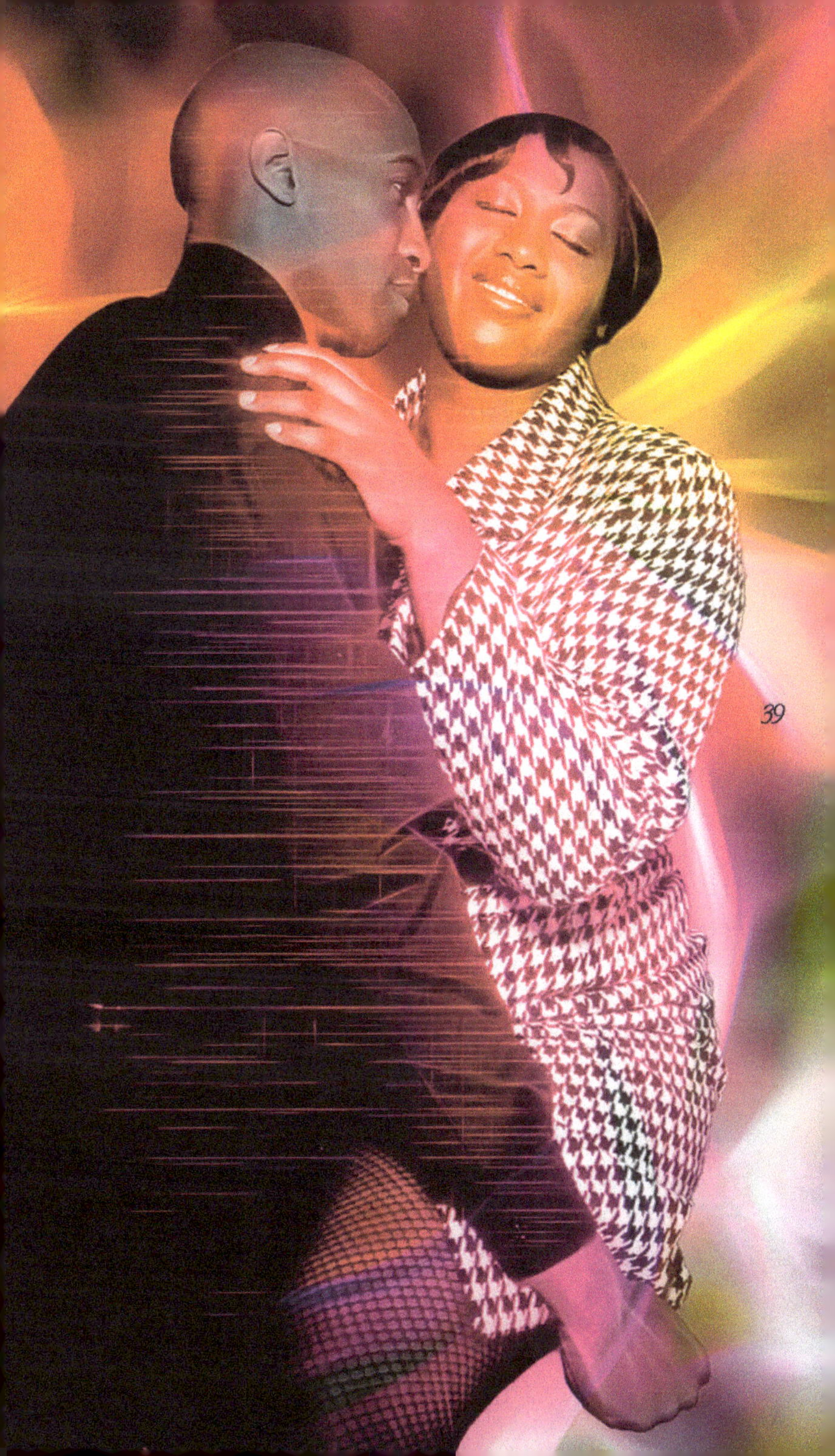

See You

I see you watching;
feel you lusting;
know you want me.

Why hold back?
Why pass me up?
Is your girl all that
to resist such an
intense connection?
You're watching me,
waiting,
wanting me to take
a secondary post.
I'm watching you back
wanting you
to make yourself
available to me --
to merge our lives in love
through body, mind, and soul.
But, you're stubborn, man;
all or nothing, that's my game.
I want you with every
fiber in me –
but my way, all the way.
Don't want to share;
not that eager
to destroy
my self-respect or
my hard-earned
sense of self.

But, I see you....

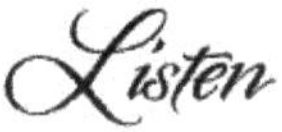

Chiseled lips sitting atop
a square jaw
chiseled, firm, delectable lips
forming a beatific smile
a sexy smirk
a boyish grin
a masculine pout.

Strong white teeth
healthy and well formed
held within healthy pink gums
closing over
a rapid, sly tongue
long and thick
muscled and seductive
succulent and enticing.

Ahh, but the words formed
by such a desirable mouth
weren't tasty morsels to savior.
Not for me.
They weren't delicacies
for my untried ear.
He spoke unpalatable words
and the only chaser offered
was his smile.

His lips formed
phrases that didn't include
commitment
relationship
monogamy

the lack of substance
in his phrases
implied lack of
honor
integrity
respect
for me
and my admiration
for him.
He was aware
of my
admiration
desire
attraction
to him.

Such undesirable words;
I am looking for
a man
a friend
a confidant
someone to share all of me with
someone with whom to build a life
to share my world
I don't need
senseless dating
casual sex
directionless partnerships.

I'm listening to his words
while being misguided
by his eyes
I'm listening to his silence
which belie what he speaks
I'm listening to my body

as it comes alive and
resonates
at his slightest touch.

I'm listening to my heart
which has deep yearnings
I'm listening to so many
clamoring sounds within and out
I deeply desire to
ignore his spoken word
and take him into me
in hopes of receiving
something more.

But at least I'm listening.

I'm listening
I'm feeling
I'm listening
I'm feeling
I'm feeling the grip of his fingers
on my buttocks as we dance
the glide of his hands
on my hips
as we pose for a photo
the embrace of his arm pulling me close
to better hear my words.

I'm listening
I'm feeling
And there's the confusion
I'm feeling....

Yearnings

I walk around dazed,
Anxious and peaked.
Yearning in many ways
To see you, touch and caress
Your body; to feel you.
Smooth back your hair,
Kiss your brow,
Glimpse your body bare.
Such sweet yearnings,
Innocent daydreams
Belying my volcanic burning.
My body is molten,
Liquid heat – with no reward.
You... can calm the burning.
You... can ignite new flames.
Caress me with your love,
Massage my depths with your sugar cane.
Swoop in and join us;
Allow me to cocoon you in my limbs -
Allow us to go beyond lust.
Let me surround you within and out;
Be your pillow and your pillar,
I expect the same, don't doubt.

When my world is quiet,
I envision you,
My mind otherwise absent.
In your eyes, I drown;
Feeling your lips,
Tasting your tongue;
Guiding your fingers
To tease and cover my breasts;

d'Ardents Désirs

J'erre atterrée
Inquiète et dépitée,
Désirant de bien des façons
Te voir, te toucher; caresser
Ton corps ; te sentir.
Lisser tes cheveux,
Embrasser ton front
Regarder la nudité de ton corps
Quels doux désirs,
Rêvasser innocemment
Le volcan qui brûle en moi
Mon corps qui fond
Chaleur liquide insatisfaite
Toi...apaise l'incendie
Toi.. qui peut raviver de nouvelles flammes
Caresse moi de ton amour
Massant mes profondeurs de ta cane à sucre.
Pénètre, pour nous joindre
Permets-moi de t'envelopper de mes membres
Que nous allions au-delà du désir.
Que je t'assaille en dedans et en dehors
Que je sois ton oreiller et ton pilier
J'en attend autant de toi, crois-moi!

Quand mon monde est silencieux
Je t'imagine,
mon esprit autrement absent
Dans tes yeux me noyant
Sentant tes lèvres
Goûtant ta langue
Guidant tes doigts
Pour que tu taquines et couvres mes seins

Capturing your hips
Between my thighs, absorbing
Your heated hardness
Into my melting pot.
My only plea, said with body, mind and soul,
"Love me. Just...love me."

Saisissant tes hanches
Entre mes cuisses
Absorbant ta dureté chaude
Dans mon four a fusion
La seule supplication de mon corps, de mon
esprit, de mon âme,
"Aime-moi...seulement aime-moi!"

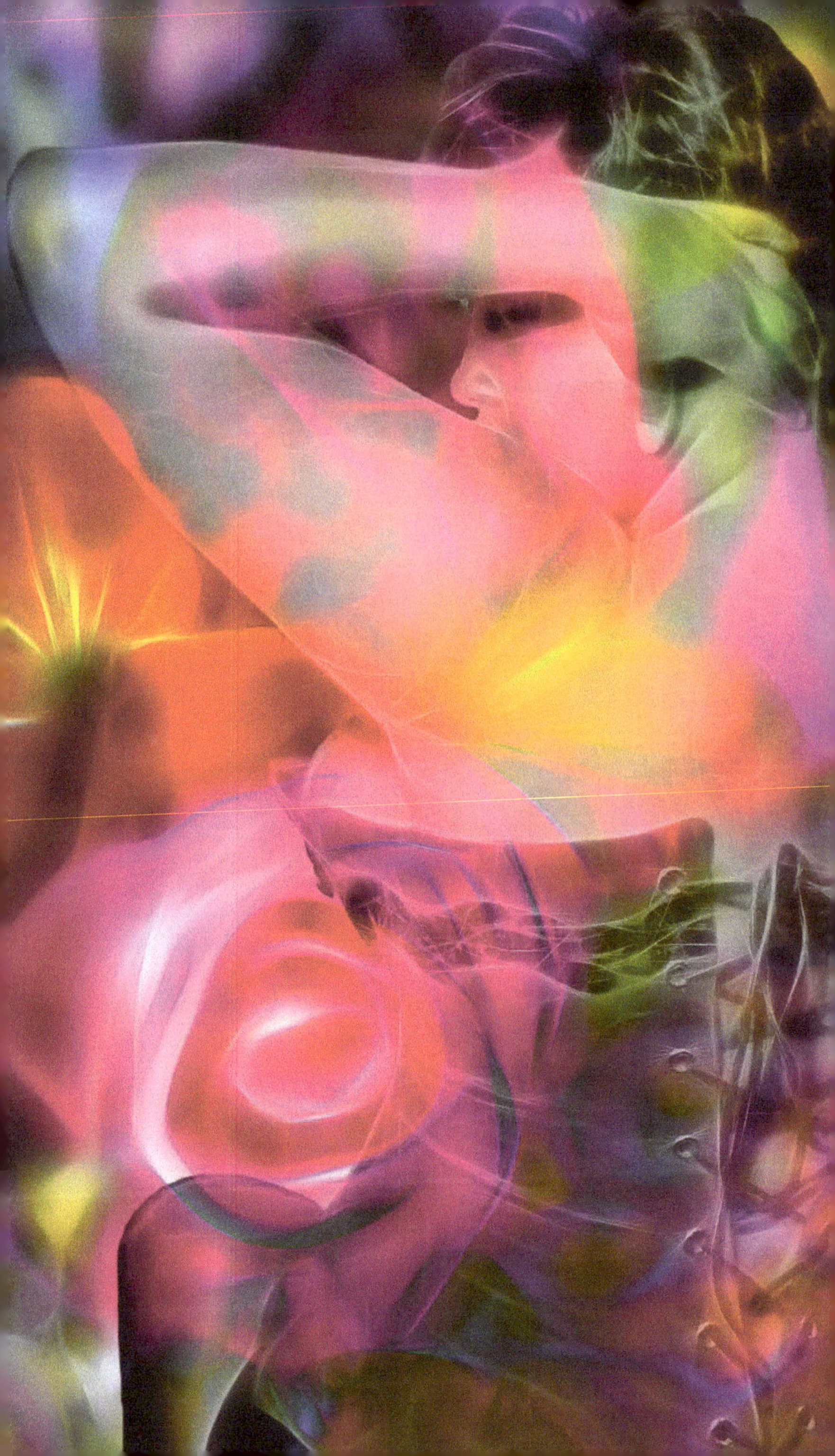

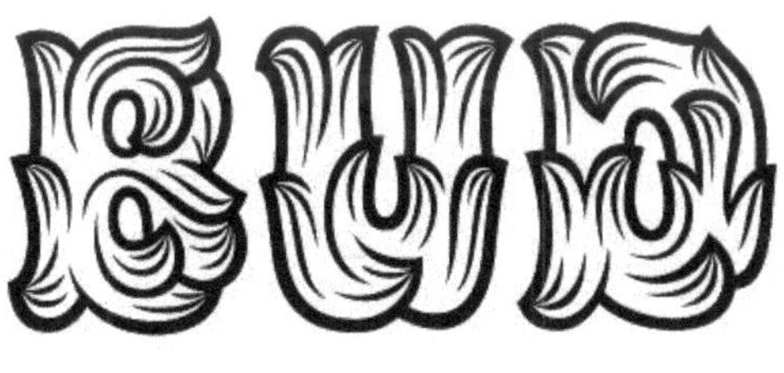

a person or thing that is not yet fully developed; to be in an undeveloped stage or condition

Suspended Fantasy

I am looking forward to
seeing another man.
He enjoys his fantasies;
he is honest about his
attraction to me.
He is sexy as hell; playfully
cocky; tall and chiseled;
witty and suggestive.
He could give you a run
for your money, simply
'cause his attention
makes me feel so good.
But lucky for you,
he's married. Already
taken, but his hugs and
rubs hint at a desire
for another possession.
My possession.
And I am tempted,
Lord, so tempted.
You are neglecting me,
ignoring me. I have
wanted you so bad for so long
and you have kept me in suspension,
albeit a very animated suspension.
Yet-in-still you outshine any man,
with just your presence,
no matter his flirtation;
no matter your indecision.

Disjointed Thoughts

discombobulated
can't walk
at work without
concentration
making coffee
thinking
the counter is
a nice height
my ass there
you between my
taunt thighs
caught
moving masterfully
in me, with me
at the gym
lifting weights
butterflies fly
as I catch a
glimpse of you
imagining you
lifting me
tossing me
yes, fucking me...
in bed at night
sleep eludes me
vivid dreams run
across my open eyes
the image, no, just
the slightest thought of
your thrusting body
moves me, shakes me
sends me...

you're over me, under me,
on me, in me,
loving me, fiercely,
tenderly, possessively,
gently, completely,
forever,
anywhere, every way
these thoughts
ravage me
as I wait
and wait,
simmer and boil
as my passion is wasted
in a lonely bed
on a lifeless tool

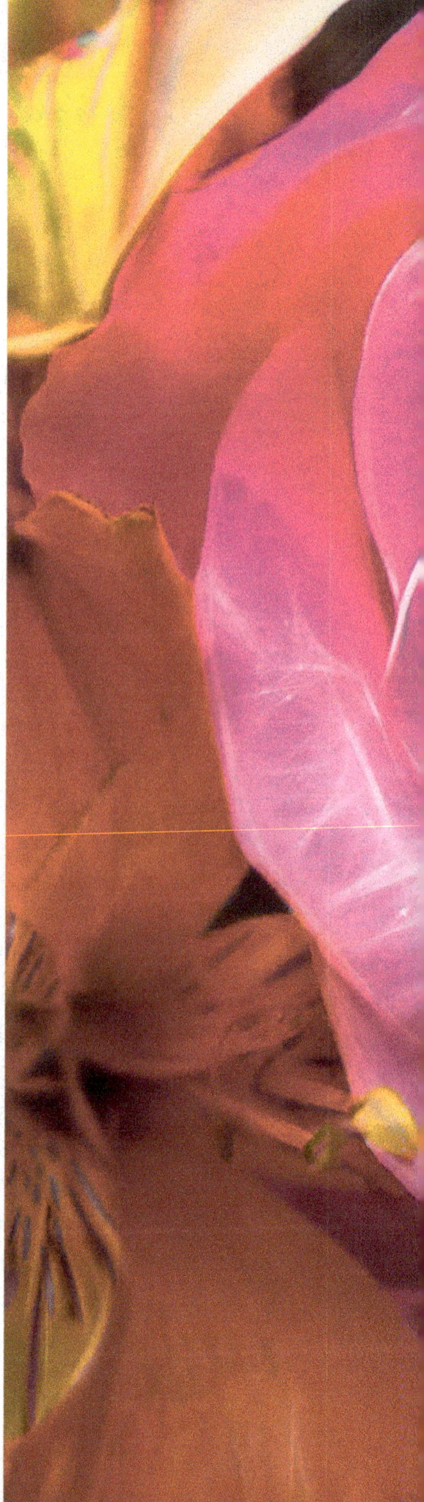

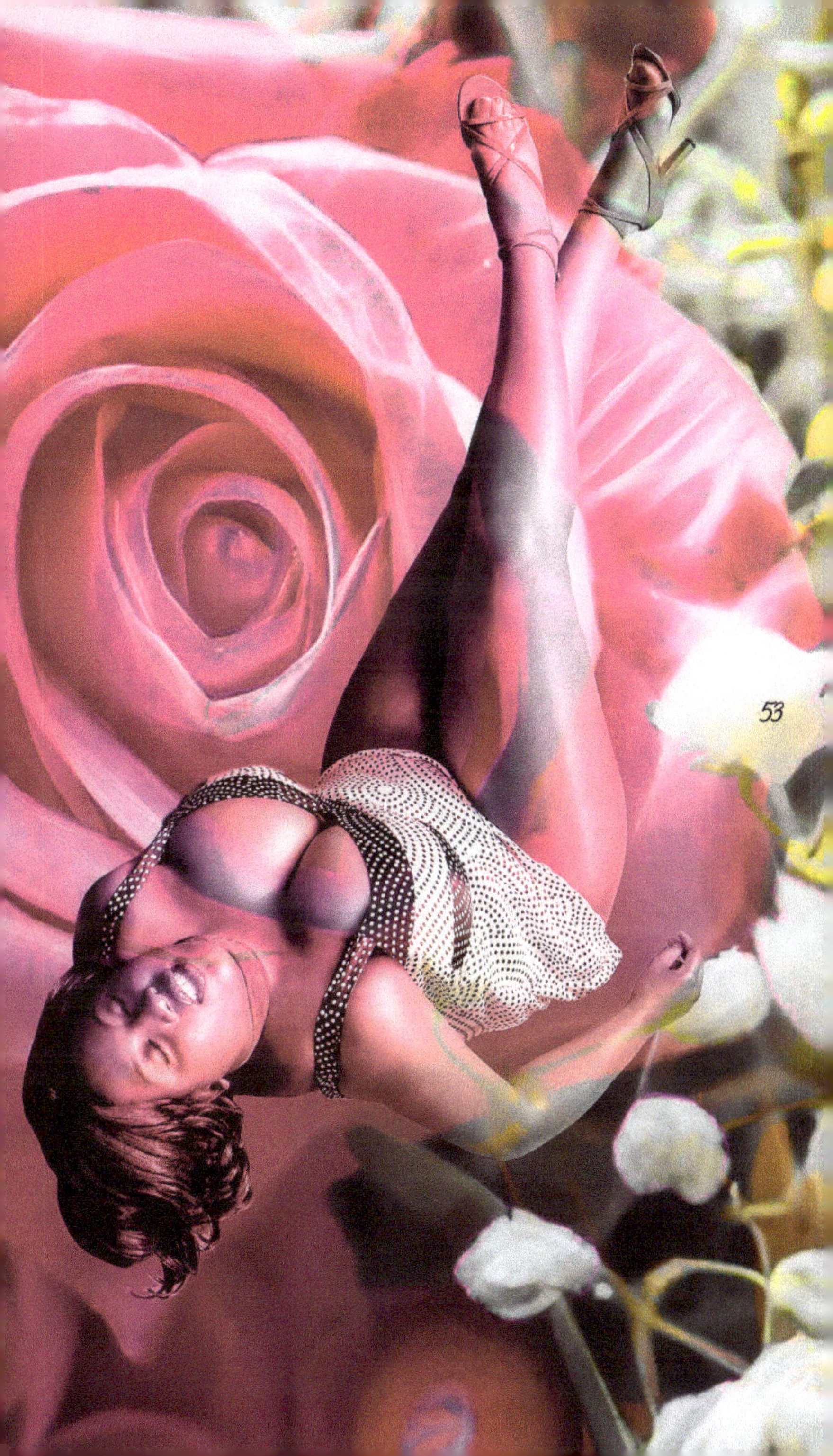

What First?

What came first
The moon or the sun;
Your stare or mine?
Did each look not blend
Seamlessly into another,
Like the sky and the sea?

Why did you lead me on
With such intensity,
Only to let me fall
Fall, fall
Slowly, clueless
Through the space
Of ignorance;
Awakened by your duplicity.
What left first?
Your interest or you;
My hope or self-respect?

Quoi en premier?

Qu'est-il venu d'abord?
La lune ou le soleil?
Ton regard ou le mien?
Chaque regard se mêlant
À l'autre sans faille
Comme le font ciel et mer?

Pourquoi m'as tu conduite
Si intensément
Pour seulement me laisser tomber
Tombe, tombe
Lentement, sans même comprendre
À travers l'espace
D'ignorance ;
Réveillée par ta duplicité.
S'en allait d'abord ?
Ton intérêt ou toi-même?
Mon espoir ou ma dignité?

Silent Way

Are you speaking to me?
Communicating
in your silent way?
I'm slow to catch
your meaning,
slow to respond,
but I hear you.
Something in me
hears your every plea.
Waiting for you
to verbalize your intent.

Are you reaching for me?
Claiming me
in your silent way?
I'm slow to reach back,
slow to acknowledge
your efforts, but I see you.
Something in me sees
deep into you.

Talk to me. just talk to me.
All you have to do
is talk to me,
and I will open this
hungry heart
and embrace you
in these loving arms
and love you from
the depths of my soul.
I'm slow to speak,
but you hear me.

Something in you
is responding to me.
Let yourself be free.
Speak to me.
Reach for me.
Claim me.

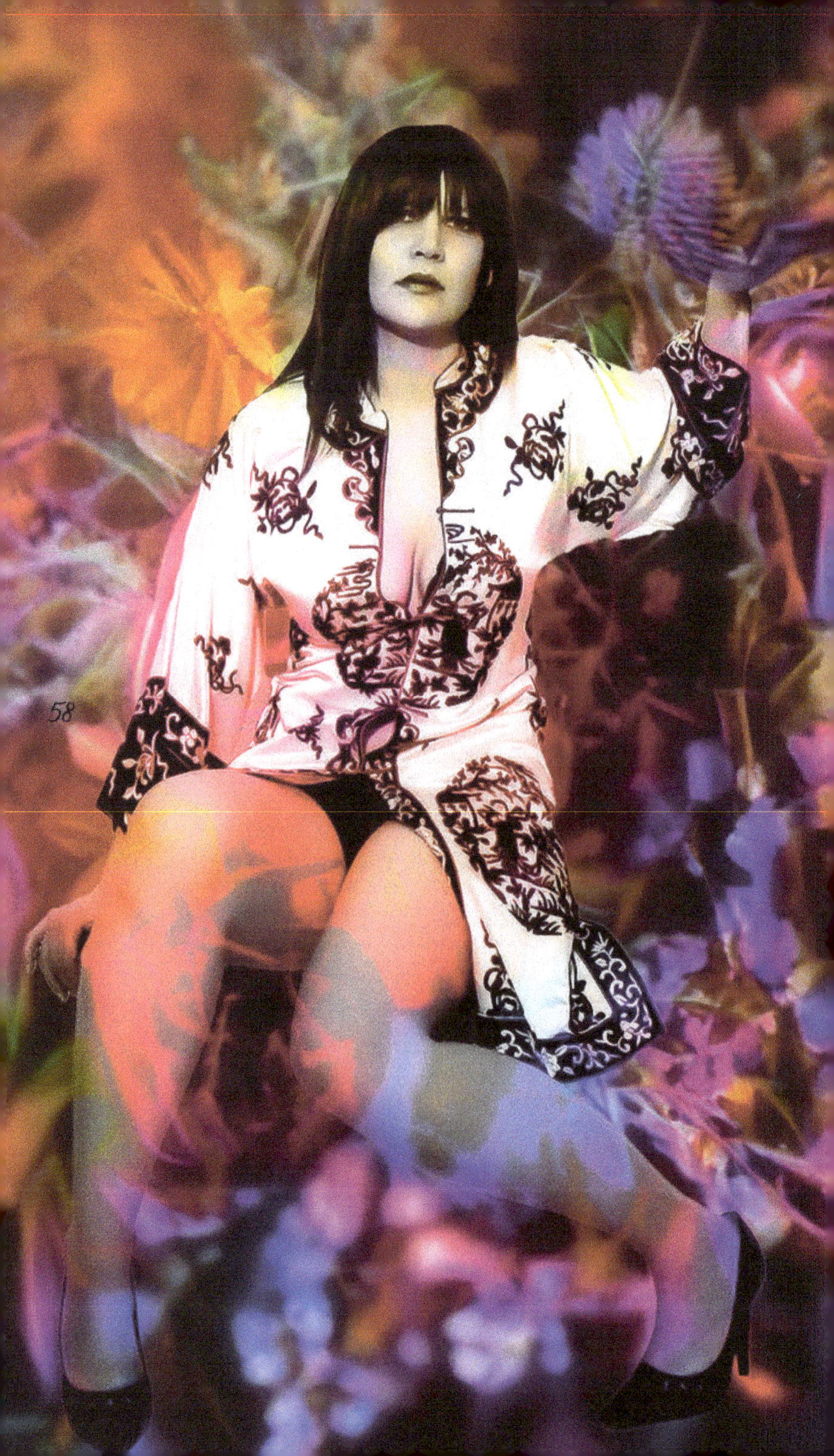

Can't Wait

Can't get you out of my head.
Goose pimples chase
one another across my skin;
nipples rise to greet you
with just a fleeting thought;
silky thighs tremble and
my creamy center
oozes with just an image
of you to stimulate me.

Can't get you off my mind.
Let go. Leave me alone.
My body is overheated –
can't sustain this
constant arousal.
Where are you?
What are you doing?
Not thinking about me,
I'm sure, otherwise we would
be one. There would be
no need to wonder at the
texture of your skin;
feel of your mouth;
weight of your body;
power of your thrust.

Can't wait to claim
your lips with mine,
to brand your body with mine.
Can't wait to consummate
my sexual ambition
and end this frustration.

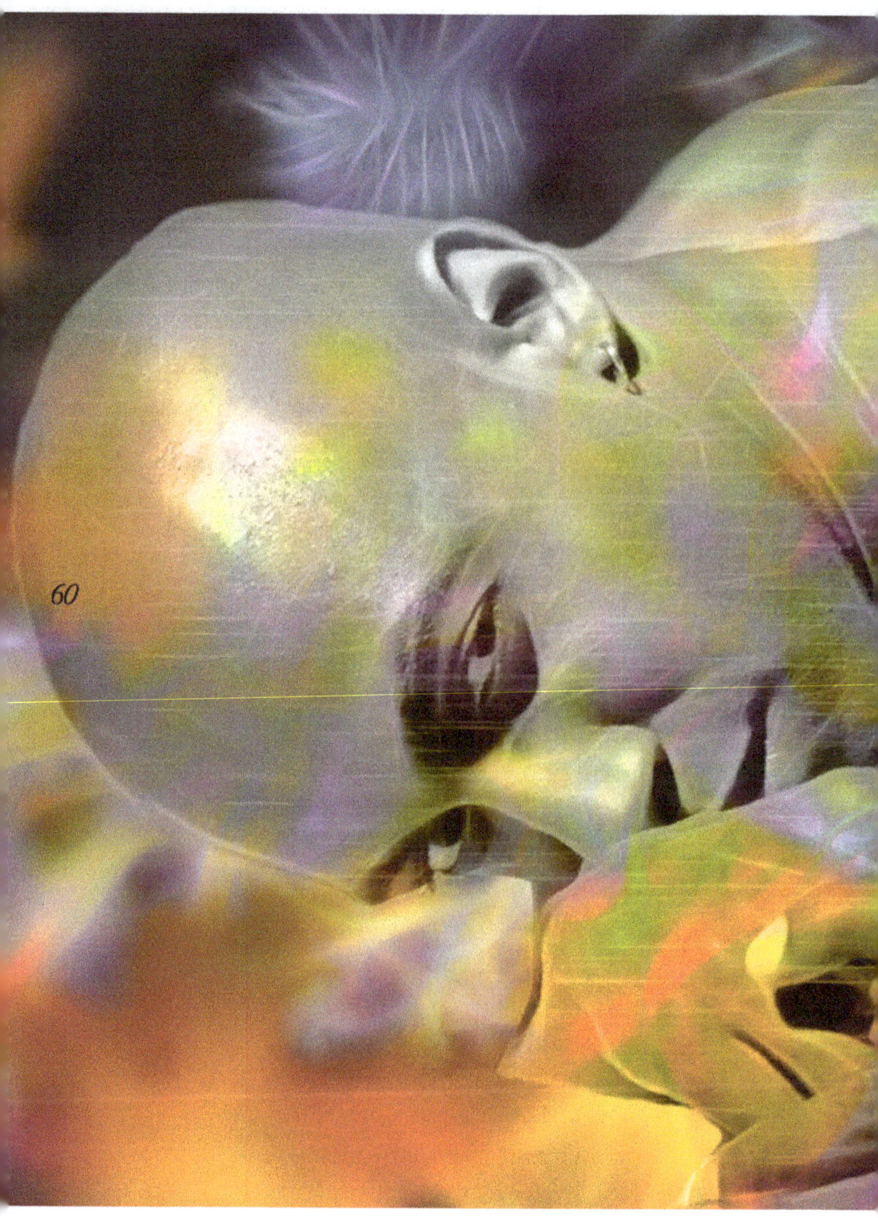

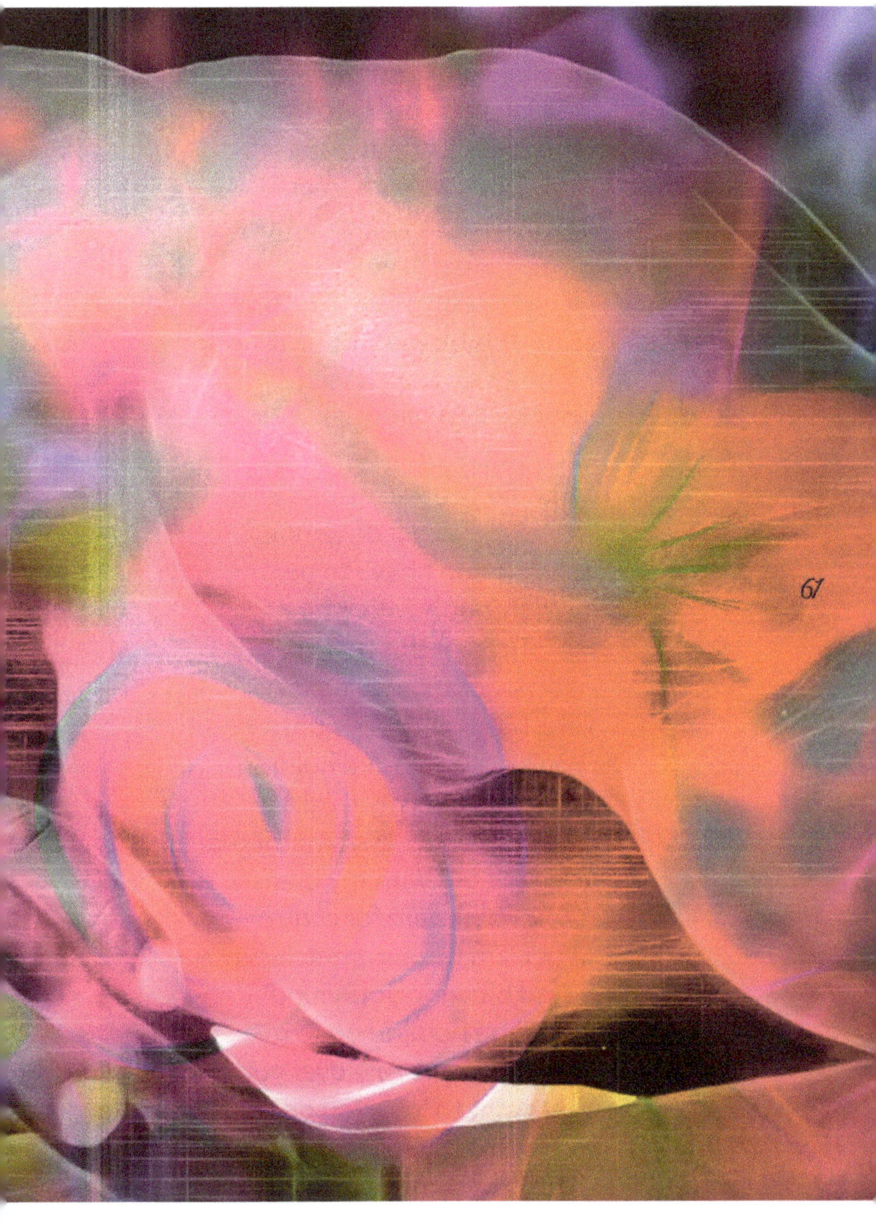

Hold On

What are you thinking?
Think I know,
As I watch you watch me.
Your eyes say you want me.
My body says it's mutual.
So why you still holding back?
You scared?
Nervous?
Intimidated?
Am I too much woman?
Or do you think you're not man enough?
Are you backing down cause
You know you will be broke off?
It's okay, luv, I'll be gentle –
You don't have to be.
But I'm through with your games,
Tired of this dance.
You want to be in control?
Fine, hold on to your power -
You'll enjoy it more holding
It between my thighs,
In the cleft of my ass, smothered
And covered with my breasts.
You won't care for control
When I'm flexing, stretching
And blowing your mind -
You'll be holding on to me.
I don't want to rule over you,
Just want to love you down.
Don't want to crush your spirit,
Just want to share mine.
Don't want all the mind games,

Just want you to rest your curly head
On my pillowy breasts.
So give in, baby. Let go.
Gather me close and hold on.

Swept Away

never thought i
would belong to another
never thought someone would
want me body and soul
don't know what your
thoughts are but regardless
my heart has been
swept away
want me or not i'm yours
waiting impatiently for your claim
body pulsing in anticipation
hypersensitive whenever
you are near
fully aware of your
ability to mentally
carry me away
don't mind the wait
sometimes
mislead to think
desires are under control
i avoid looking at you
while you
avoid looking at me
then you strut and prance
for me and again, I am
swept away

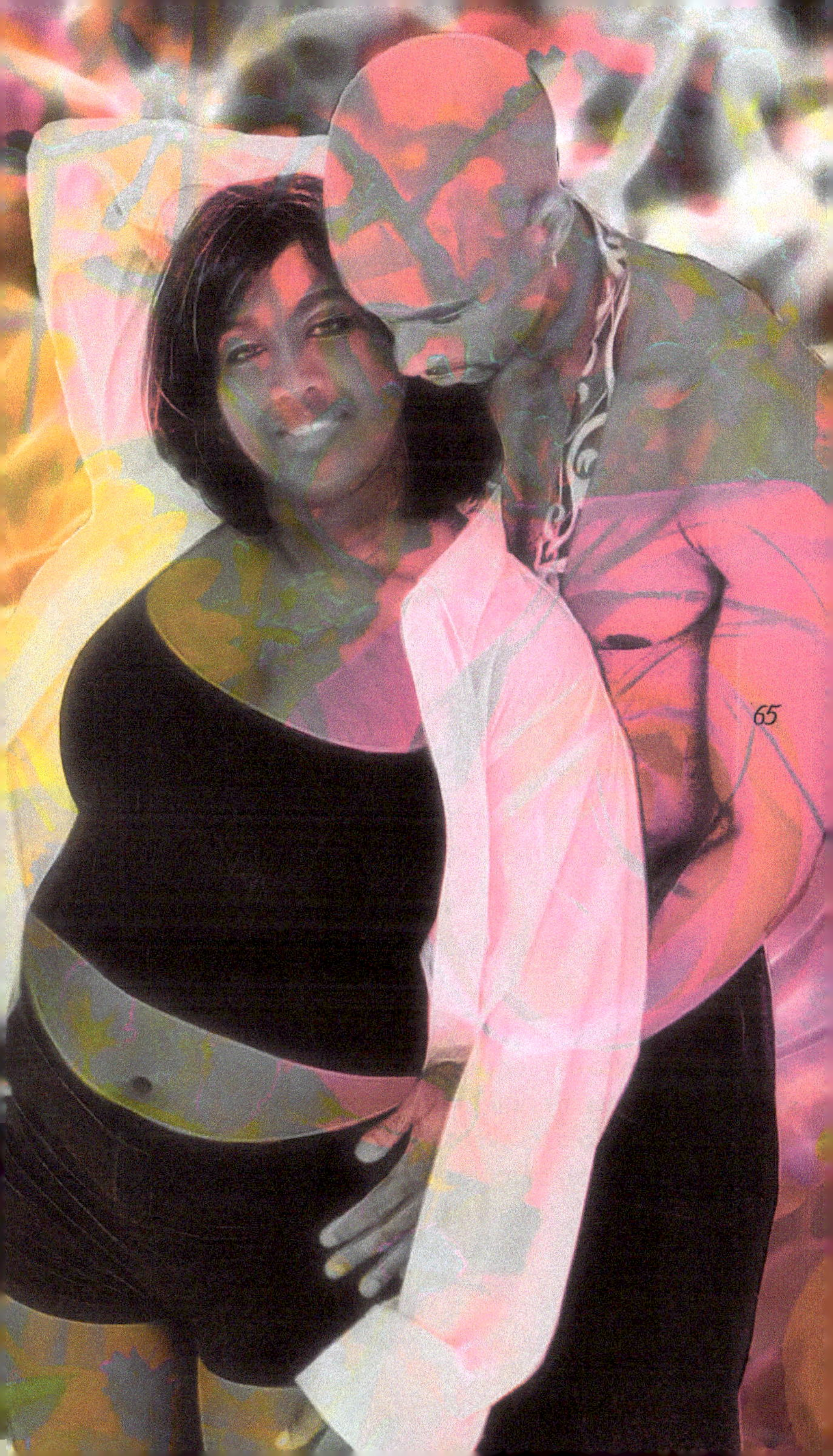

Dream Lover

I have a lover who visits me every night.
A faithful, talented, attentive lover
who keeps me excited through the day.
Ah! This lover is a wonder to behold,
so beautiful, earnest and bold.
Piercing dark eyes, straight patrician nose
posed over the most *de-li-cious* lips.

Mmmm.... Succulent molded lips
explore every hypersensitive inch of my body;
resting to nibble in the dips and valleys;
continuing with a leisurely suckle at each peak.
My lover allows me to be all
my imagination can conjure,
true to him, myself and the
primitive call of my senses.
Nothing is too rough or too kinky.
Never too soft or too lingering.
Always right, tight with pitch perfect friction
Sychronized motion to give and receive all we
can

Ohhh.... He commands my senses,
this warrior of my loins, conqueror of my body.
Skin to skin he let's me in.
Solicits my opinion, courts my conversation.
He voices his woes and shares his goals.
This lover of mine shares his dreams.
He holds me tight through the loving
and keeps me close through the night.

I Just Wanna

I just wanna make love to you
That's it
No fuss
Perhaps a whole lot of mess
Rocking, rolling, sucking, soothing
Bliss
Bliss
Bliss

I just wanna share joy with you
That's all
No complications
Just a whole lot of laughter
Openness, deepness, sharing, caring
Smile
Smile
Smile

I just wanna smile again
Nothing more
No guile or hiding
Only carefee, deep-rooted, nerve-tingling,
goose-pimpling, stomach-quivering
Love
Love
Love

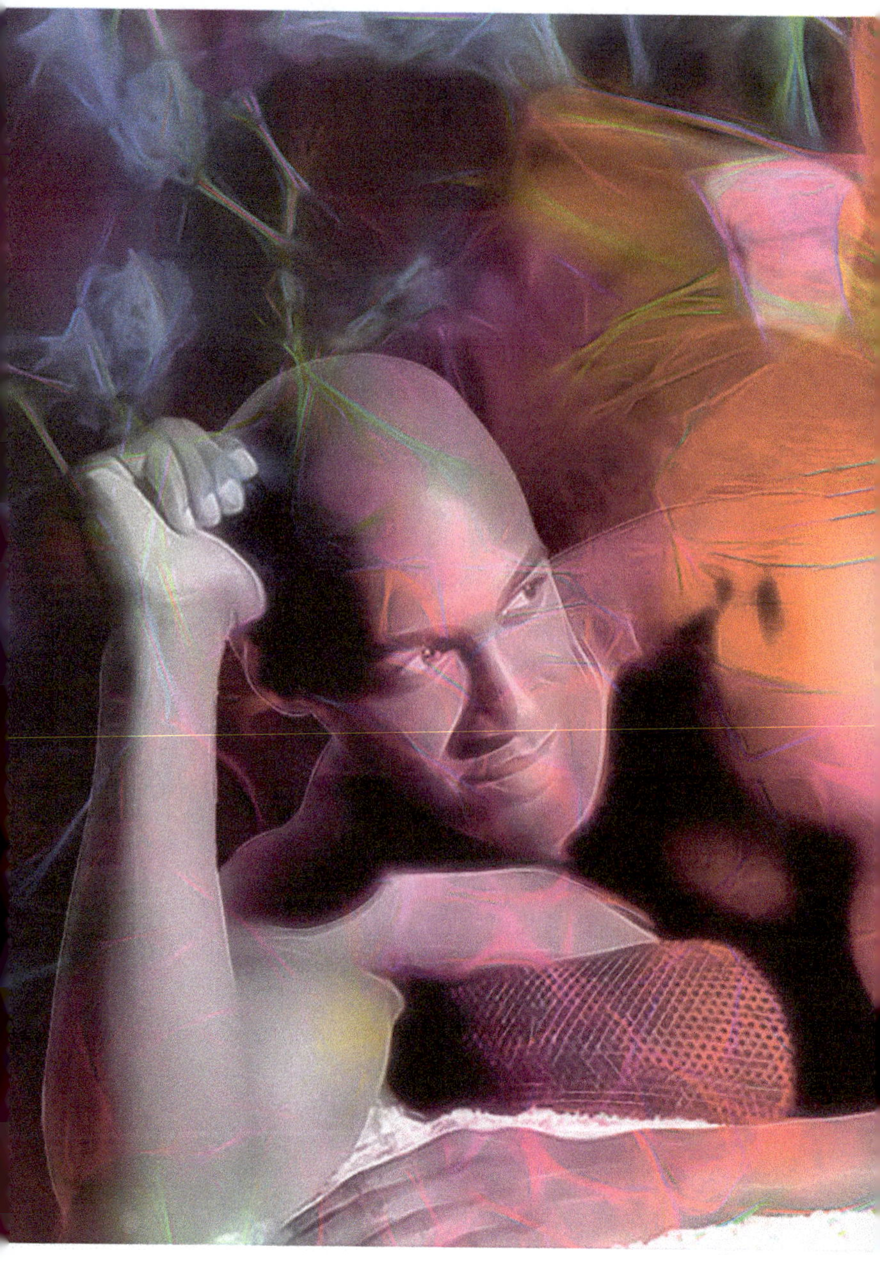

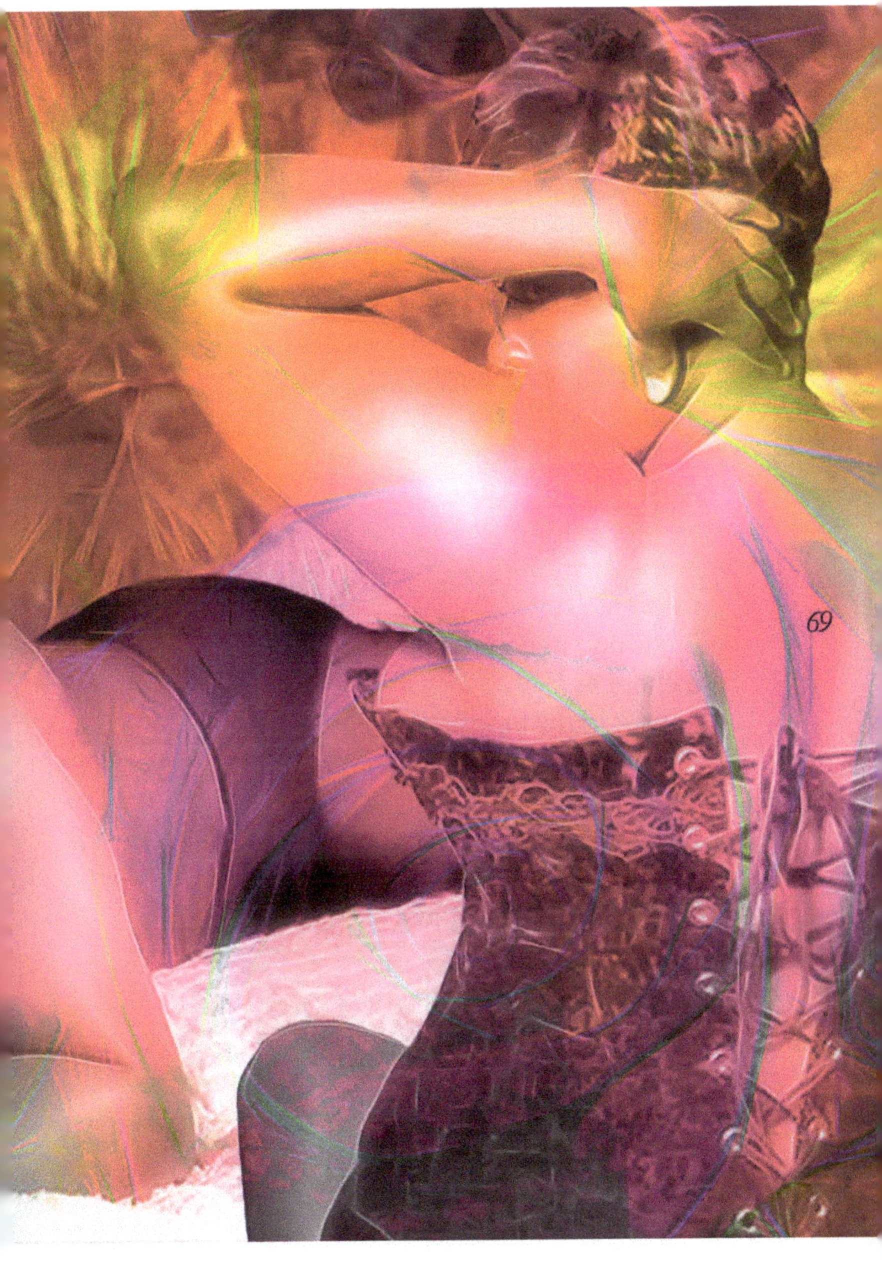

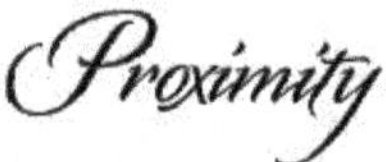

Words cannot express
the effect you have on me.
Passing within inches
of your body
leaves me anxious, excited,
breathless....
Coming in contact with
your eyes,
Oh, Lord, have mercy!
Your whole countenance
is simply a wonder to behold!
Words are foreign
to my mouth;
coherency, foreign
to my mind.
Breathing becomes
a chore as air
pauses in my lungs.
All this....
You shut down my body
with just your proximity.
You didn't send a smile my way,
didn't brush against me;
no, not the slightest
meeting of our flesh –
and all this....
Just being near you –
despite my resolve to
ignore you, to move on
to a man with sincere
interest in me –
just being close to you

La Proximité

Les mots ne peuvent exprimer
ton effet sur moi.
Passer si près
de ton corps
me laisse inquiète, enthousiaste,
etonnée….
Approchant le contact
de tes yeux
Oh, seigneur, de grâce!
Toute ton expression
est simplement merveille à contempler!
Les mots manquent
à ma bouche;
la cohérence, étrangère
à mon esprit.
Respirer devient
pesant lorsque l'air
s'arrête dans mes poumons.
Tout ça....
Tu paralyses mon corps
à ta seule proximité.
Tu n'as pas souri vers moi
Tu ne tes pas frotté contre moi ;
non, même pas la moindre
rencontre de notre chair –
et tout ça....
Être simplement près de toi
malgré ma décision
de t'ignorer, de passer
à un autre qui sincèrement
s'intéressera à moi –
être près de toi

puts a wobble in my knees,
a flutter in my belly,
an extra swing to my hips
(a come hither gyration you didn't heed),
seeming wings to my heart
as it soared at speed
away from rational thought,
a shake to my head as I wondered
at the effect your mere pro-xi-mi-ty
has on me. You leave me breathless....

Yet, for all this, you
gave me buoyancy. So
much I couldn't contain myself.
Left the gym to release my yelps
and screeches in the welcome
privacy of my car. Your proximity
gives me such a high, I have a
joyful fear of becoming
addicted to your touch.

fait trembler mes genoux
fait battre mon ventre
un peu plus osciller mes hanches
(déhanchement t'incitant tu n'en tenais pas compte),
mon coeur semble avoir des ailes
alors qu'il s'élève rapidement
loin de la réalité
secouant la tête émerveillée
à l'effet de ta pro-xi-mi-té.
Tu me laisses essoufflée....

Oui, pour tout ça
tu me fit exubérante. Tellement
exubérante que je ne pouvais me contenir.
laissant la gym pour mes cris
et gémissements dans l'intimité
opportune de ma voiture. Ta proximité
m'exalte tant que j'ai une
crainte heureuse de devenir
adonnée de ton toucher.

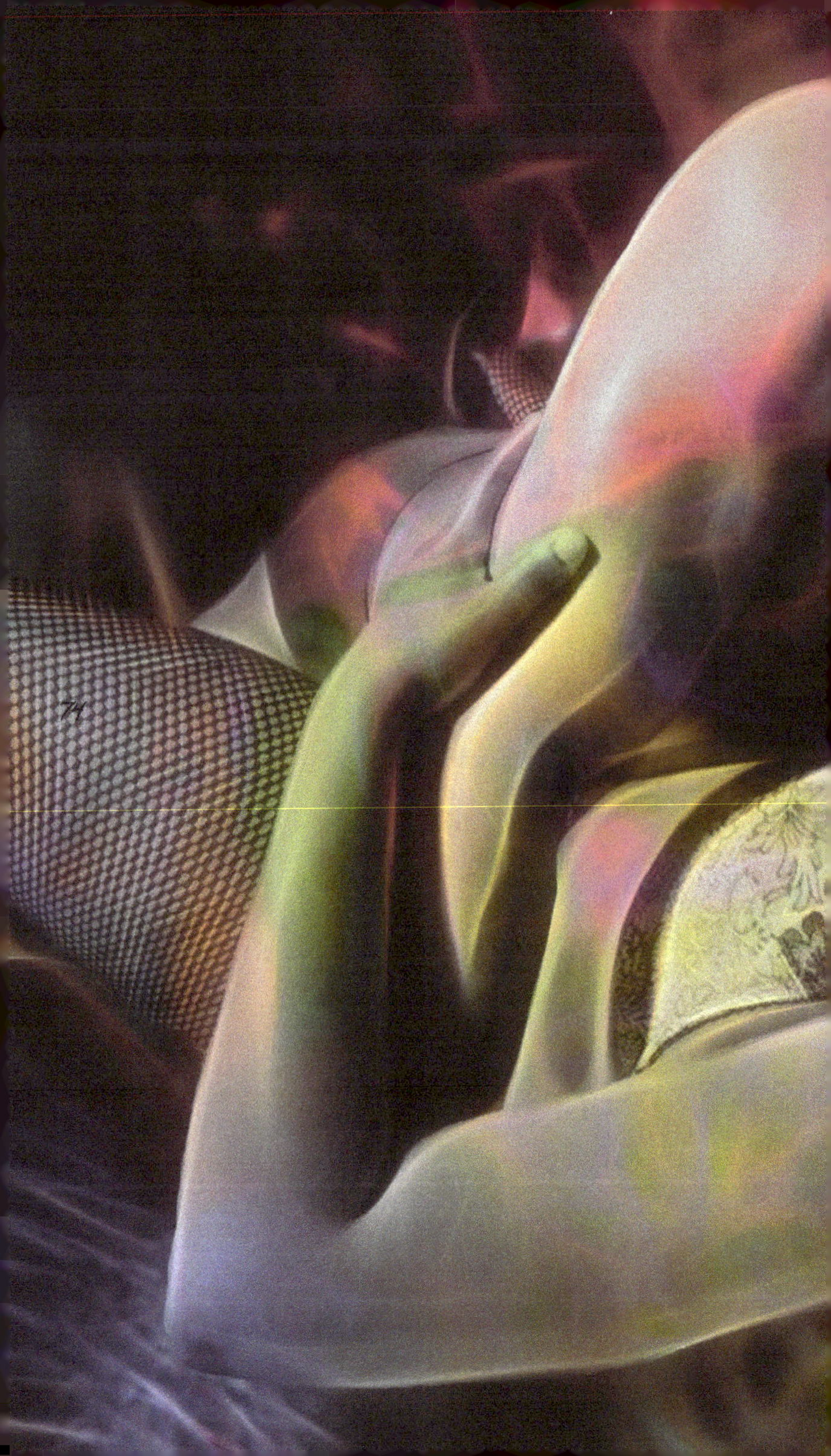

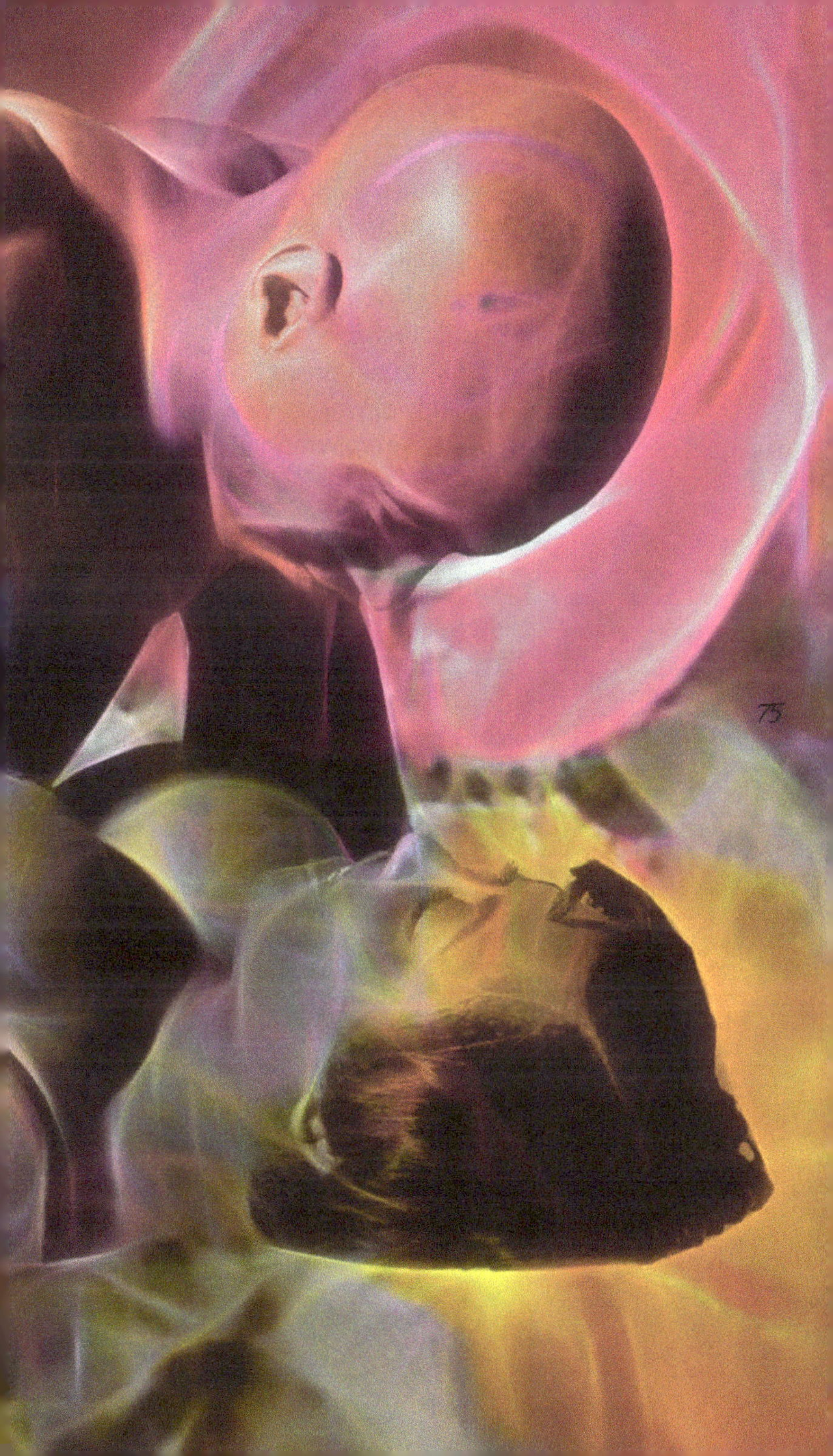

You Are

you are my light
my sunshine
my joy, my ambition
you are all of my hope
all I dream of
my fantasies consist
only of you
friends say I'm wrong
they say I'm clueless
I'm crazy
to be so devoted
so caught up in feelings
when I can't get even
a greeting from you
regardless, all I want
all I need you are

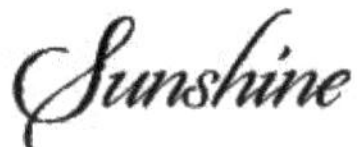

Amazing
Spectacular
Beautiful
Glorious
Sunshine
Warming me
Inspiring me
Attracting me
Luring me
To bask in your
Sultry rays

Your hot
Sensuous
Beauty
Blinds me

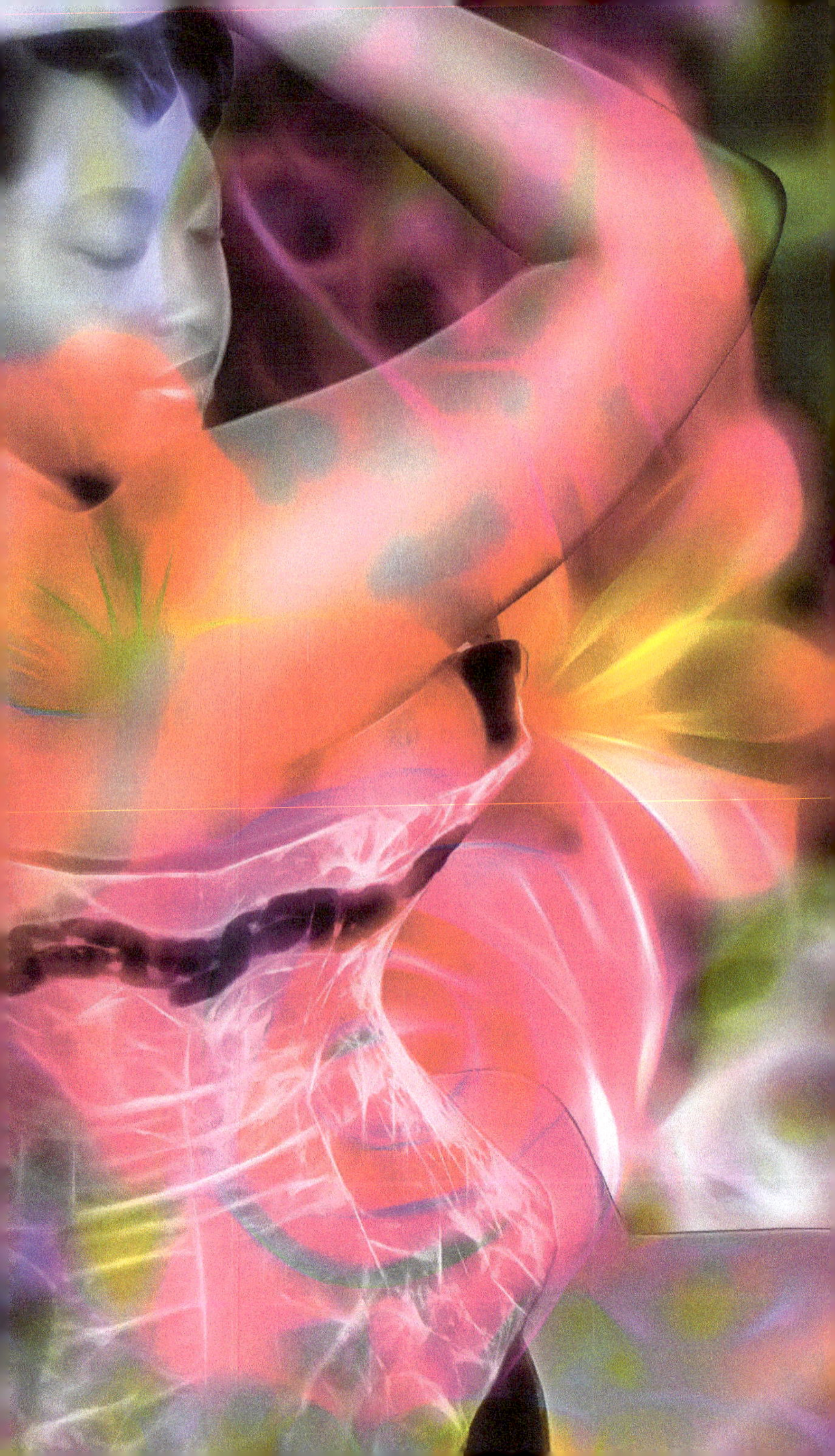

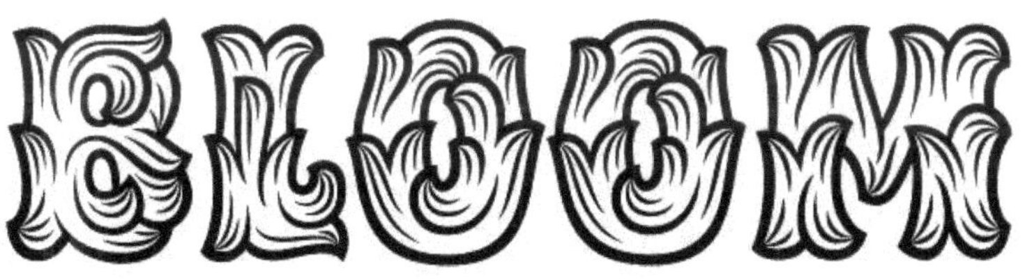

The condition of being in flower; a condition or time of vigor and beauty. Prime.

seed, Bud, BLOOM

Living in the shadow of fear
Loving deeply but only in secret
Planning a lifetime never to be shared
Up till now, this has been my life
So much hoped for
So little realized

Now, my courage is unfurling
Reaching deep to root in my spirit
Determination is blooming
Springing forth to frame my reality
Love has morphed into a conflagration
Of lust and back again

Once a seed
Love sprouted buds
Beautifully fragile blooms
Fragrant with sexual anticipation
Tense with expectations
Eager to savor
Its own sweetness
And bear its own fruit

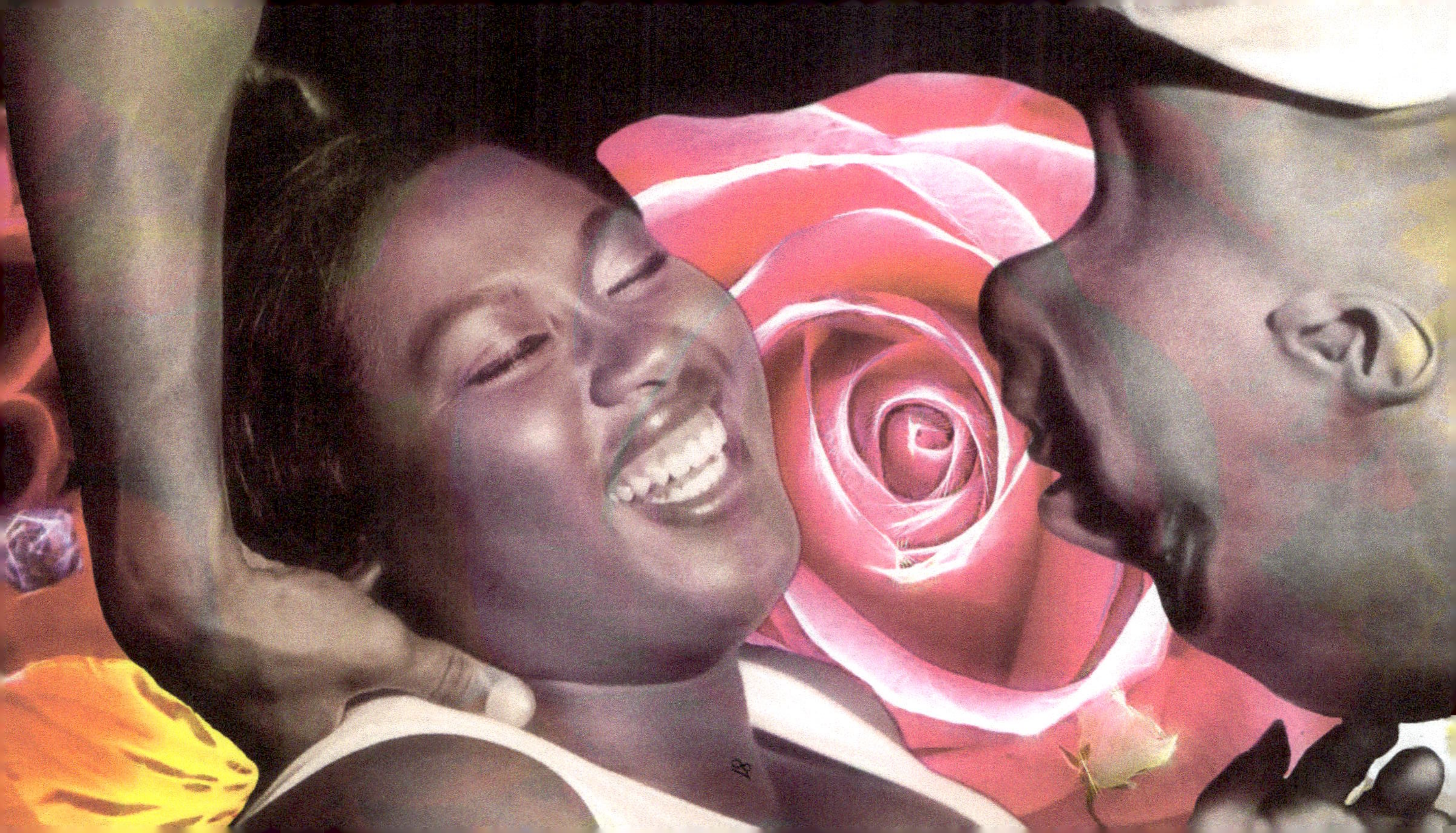

Wake You

I want to wake you
with my mouth
I want to straddle your
hard muscle-strewn thighs
and stroke you into awareness
my breath warming you

I can see you so clearly –
peacefully asleep
your dark curly head
resting on my lilac pillows
your sensuous lips slightly
parted as you breathe in our
mingled scent
your long beautiful body
spread out like the most
inviting, delectable feast

I want to wake you
with my tongue
I can taste you now
my nose nuzzling
your member
as my lips trail your
thickening veins
I can feel you
hardening, lengthening
against my tongue as I take
you into the heated
early-morning moistness of my mouth
I want to feel you blossom
between my lips and jerk

against my tongue

I want to wake you
with my teeth
lightly, ever so gently
moving down the length
of your shaft

and coming back up again
accompanied by my
soothing, lapping tongue;
At last your girth
is too great for the
casing of my mouth
so I begin licking you up,
down, and around
like the grandest
tastiest and most succulent
of lollipops.

Wake You Too

Thinking about waking you
with my tongue,
mmmm, what a thought.
Certainly not meant to limit
myself or your pleasure
I wish to wake you every
morning with a new sensation.
This morning I wake you with
the tips of my breasts
trailing your chest
circular motions, figure-eights
I want to map out your every
skin-cell with the hungry
eyes of my areolas.
I want my breasts to weep
with glee as they press
against your well-defined pecs.
You'll embrace me in
your sleep, instinctively
fitting every angle
to every curve.
My thighs spread eagerly
to straddle your arching hips,
encasing your sugarcane
within my honeyed walls.

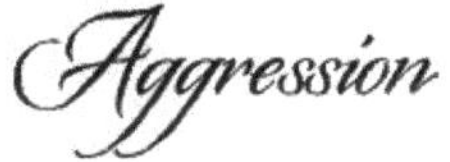

got a jones
an itch
you need to scratch
tension raise my
nipples
frustration demands
a rub down
running weeping
hands along my body
envisioning you
feeling your
large firm hands
gripping
my ass
lifting and separating
pulling me in
pressing my ache
to your throbbing penis
your white tee
rips apart between
anxious fingers
exposing your
bare torso to
hungry lips
nipping teeth
lapping tongue
desire to be dominated
gives way to a
compulsion to ravish

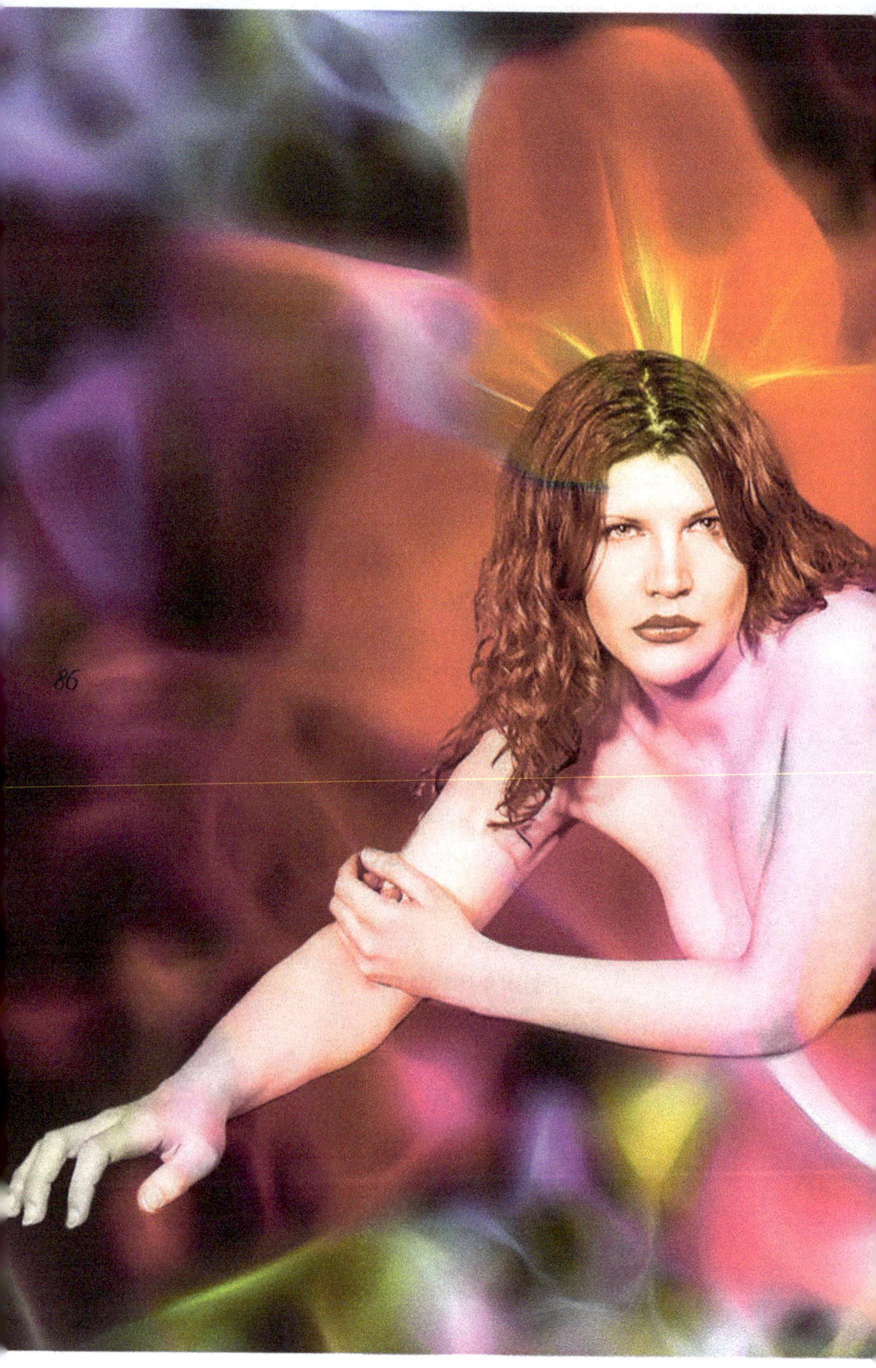

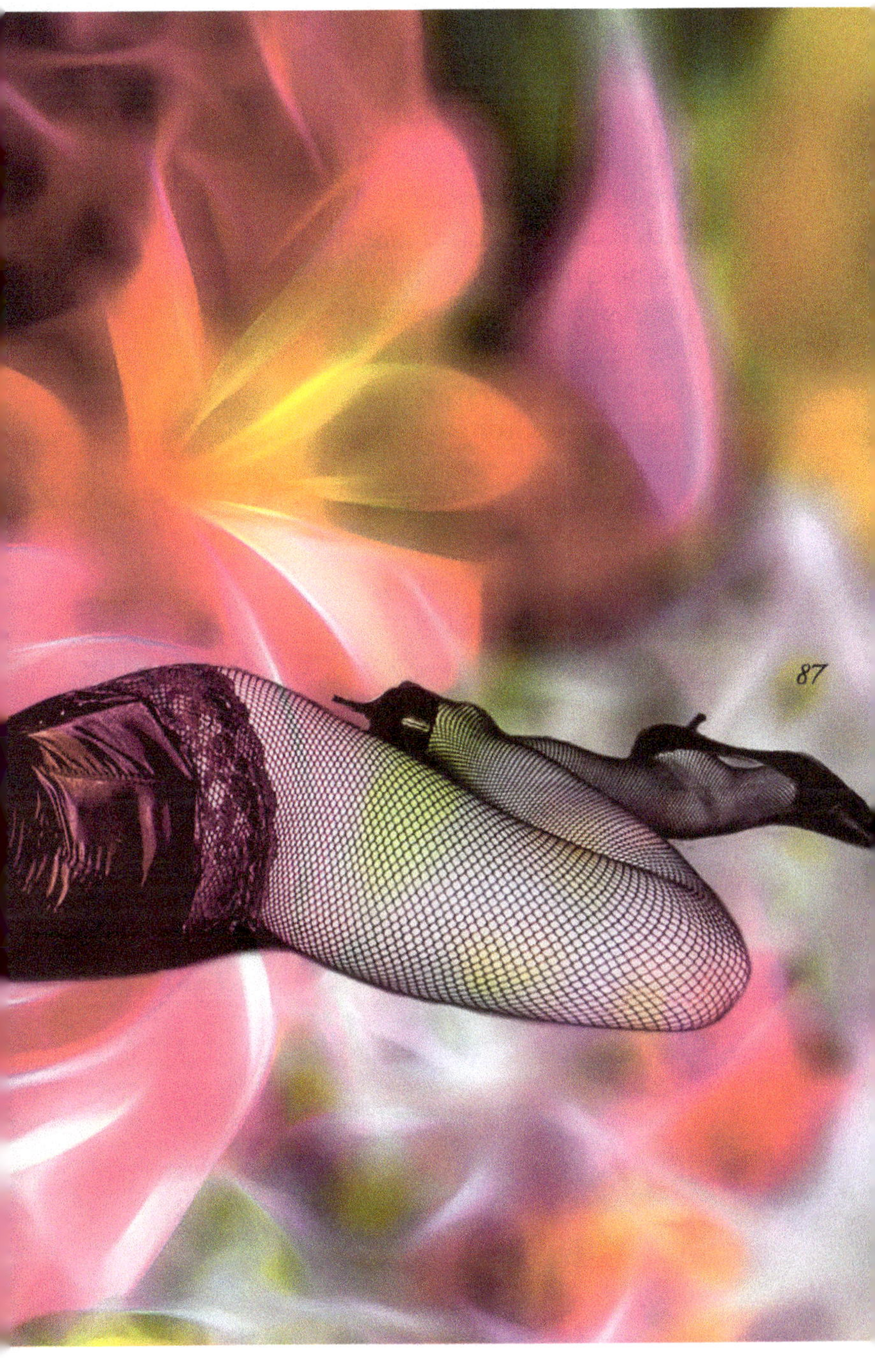

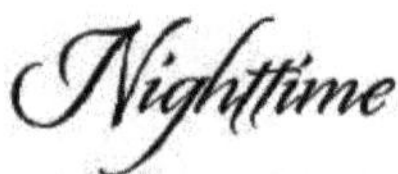

Struggled through my day
with you as my motivation.
In bed sending myself to sleep
with images of your smile.
Calming my body with the
promise of your possession.
I've done so much to prepare
for you, my body no longer
holds secrets from me
I'm ready to explore you.
Dreams are no longer enough;
I'm ready to be yours.
You dominate my senses –
now, come claim all of me.

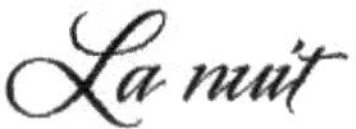

Ayant lutté toute la journée
avec toi comme motivation.
Au lit, je m'endors
avec des images de ton sourire.
Apaisant mon corps avec
la promesse de ta possession.
J'ai tant fait pour t'être prête
mon corps ne me
retenant plus de secrets.
Je suis prête à t'explorer.
Les rêves ne suffisant plus;
je suis prête à être tienne.
Tu domines mes sens –
maintenant, viens réclamer tout de moi.

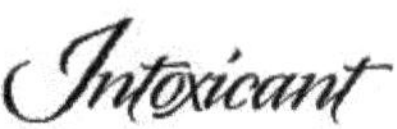

Intoxicant

I drifted fitfully to sleep
last night with your image before me
in the night.

Your presence was so strong
you could've been there with me.
Your demanding
intoxicating body in my bed,
between my legs. My thighs
braced on your shoulders.
Your face blended into my
earthy environment. Your nose
nestled against my blossoming bud
as your hungry, devouring mouth
opened over my nether lips.
Oh! The rush of feeling....
My body jerked,
back arched, head fell back –
hit the wall, actually, as I tried to
pull away from the onslaught of
intoxicating sensations....
Didn't want to let go – too scared to be free.
I pulled my core away, only to have you
follow my retreat. Your nose inched
closer, as your tongue dove deeper.
Your mouth consumed more as your hands
clutched my buttocks to hold your
nourishment in place.
I loved every moment, every second.
Loved your grip, your possession.
Loved every lap and thrust of your
intoxicating tongue.
So blissfully divine.

I laid there, eyes wide shut,
staring blindly, seeing everything in the
darkness of the night – feeling, experiencing
you. My body twitched and jerked,
trembled and arched with every
imagined move you made.

Finally, I let go of my fear and a tidal
wave of pleasure overtook me.
I don't know if I spoke the words,
but *"I need you"* looped through my mind.
Even if my shy, trembling whispers
didn't reach you, my screaming, bucking
body
did. Suddenly, you surged up to cover
my aching breasts with your massive chest.
Your mouth claimed mine and I tasted
the aroma and juices you had feasted on.
Such an exotic, cloying musk.
Such an intoxicating, full-bodied taste.
Your tongue, your lips, your mouth
gave my essence back to me
as your body plunged into my overflowing
vessel.
Your power electrified me, elevated me,
multiplied us.
Our union brought the peace I sought –
I sank limply into the mattress, giving
up consciousness for satiated rest.

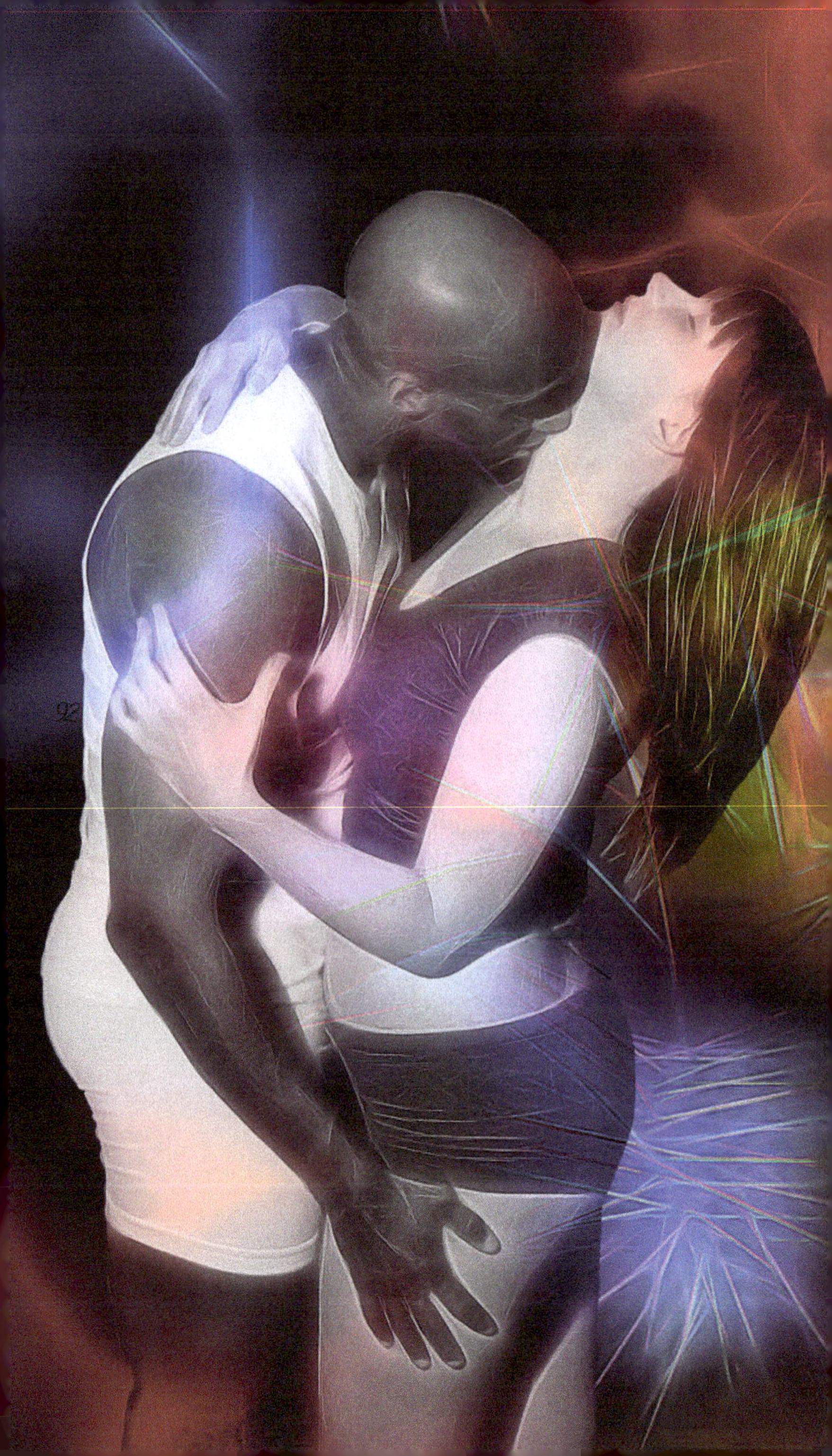

You

Waiting for your arms
your hands
your fingers
Waiting for your embrace
your grip
your caress

Longing for your lips
your teeth
your tongue
Longing for your smile
your nibble
your kiss

Imagining your girth
your length
your rhythm
Imagining your homecoming
your welcome
your endurance

Wanting you
More of you
All of you
Now, always, indefinitely

Wake Me

Last night, I dreamed a dream
I slept a peaceful cocooned sleep in your arms.
Last night, I kissed your lips
before resting my head next to yours.
Your arms encircled my waist,
your hand cupped my breast
as you pulled me into your chest.
As comfortable as this position was,
I wanted to drift to sleep with you
enveloped in my limbs.
Before sliding into oblivion,
I remember rolling over to drape my thigh over your hip,
I slid my arm beneath yours to rub your back,

I remember resting my face in the crook of your neck;
my senses soothed by your scent.
My transition dislodged your soothing hand
from the bounty of my breast.
But, my darling, you are ever so resourceful;
your beloved hand slid down my silken back to
rest comfortably on the high curve of my derrière.

This morning I awoke spellbound.
I drifted into awareness on clouds of joy.
Your chest moved with the breathing rhythm of your sleep
but part of you was rampantly awake,
proposing a slow morning loving.
As you eased into wakefulness, you eased into me,
and that dream I dreamed became reality.

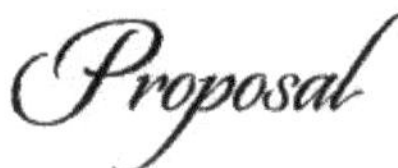

Proposal

Just sitting here thinking
about the possibility of us.
So wrapped up in my thoughts;
out of my mind crazy, friends say.
Not so, not quite.
Why are you so difficult?
All you have to do is follow-through.
Less is needed from you than you think.
Love, laughter and partnership I offer;
ever faithful, I promise –
never would I stray.

My Sun

Glory, glory, hallelujah!
The reverberating crescendo
of a gospel choir
moves through me
when I see you.
Just to see you
grants me light,
vision, buoyancy.
You are a ray unlike
any other.
The electricity of your presence,
the heat of your aura
beckons me, energizes
me, mesmerizes me.
I am as a moth
drawn to your magnetic flame;
basking in the scorching
burn of your essence.
And your heat isn't
a mild, comfortable thing.
It doesn't merely warm my skin
and grant me a soft glow
from this distance.
Your heat encapsulates me;
pulses through my veins;
boils my blood. It causes an
ebb and flow from my core –
for so long, thought
to be barren, desolate, impenetrable –
my core is like molten
lava ready to erupt;
ready to conquer and

Mon Soleil

Gloria, gloria, alléluia!
Le crescendo résonnant
d'une chorale gospel
me transperce
quand je te vois.
Juste te voir
m'accorde lumière,
vision, suspension.
Tu es un rayon comme
aucun autre.
L'électricité de ta présence,
la chaleur de ton aura
me guide, me nourrit,
me captive.
Tel un papillon de nuit
qu'attire ta magnétique flamme ;
m'offrant à l'ardeur brûlante
de ton essence.
Et ta chaleur n'est
ni légère, ni agréable.
Ne réchauffant simplement pas ma peau
aucune douce lueur
ne lui vient de ce lointain.
Ta chaleur m'emprisonne;
battant dans mes veines;
à faire bouillir mon sang.
Le flux et reflux de mon cœur –
que je pensais si longtemps
aride, dévasté, impénétrable –
mon coeur est de lave en fusion
prêt à jaillir;
prêt à conquérir et

cover you with my glowing
embers; ready to embrace you
and create a slate for new life.
You are my sun. You breathe
new life into me each
time I see you.

I bask in the glow of your aura;
simmer in the heat of your gaze;
my skin comes alive at the
nearness of your passing.
You invigorate me, inspire me.
You bring me to life.
Amen.

à te couvrir de braises ardentes,
prêt à t'étreindre et
à réécrire la vie.
Tu es mon soleil. Tu renouvelle
la vie en moi chaque
fois que je te vois.

Je m'offre à l'ardeur brûlante de ton essence;
frémissant à la chaleur de ton regard;
ma peau revit
à l'approche de ton passage.
Tu me fortifies, tu m'inspire.
Tu me ravives.
Amen.

Understanding "Night Time"

"Night time is the right time
to be with the one you love."
Ray said it with such feeling...
"to beeee with the one you love, now...."

Prior to you I did not
understand such raw emotion,
such desperate yearning. Such a
desire to supplicate oneself to another.
I had never experienced tremors
coursing through my body as
a song reverberated through my soul;
while thoughts of a man heated my blood.

I imagine at some point
Margie fell to her knees to
illustrate her devotion to Ray
as she belted out,
"Baby, Baby, Baby, oh Baby---
Do I love you? No one above you.
Hold me tight,
And make everything alright."
I hear pain and strength
in her voice. Devotion and
pleading. Love and urgency.
Her words shake me.
Then I imagine you as I accompany
Margie's demanding verse,
"Tease me, squeeze me, leave me...
Oh, don't leave me. Oh, Baby.
Take my hand, now.
I don't need no other man."

Night time, this life time is
the right time to be with the one
you love. Just want you to
love me, need me, hold me
just *be* with me.
Oh, baby, just be with me.

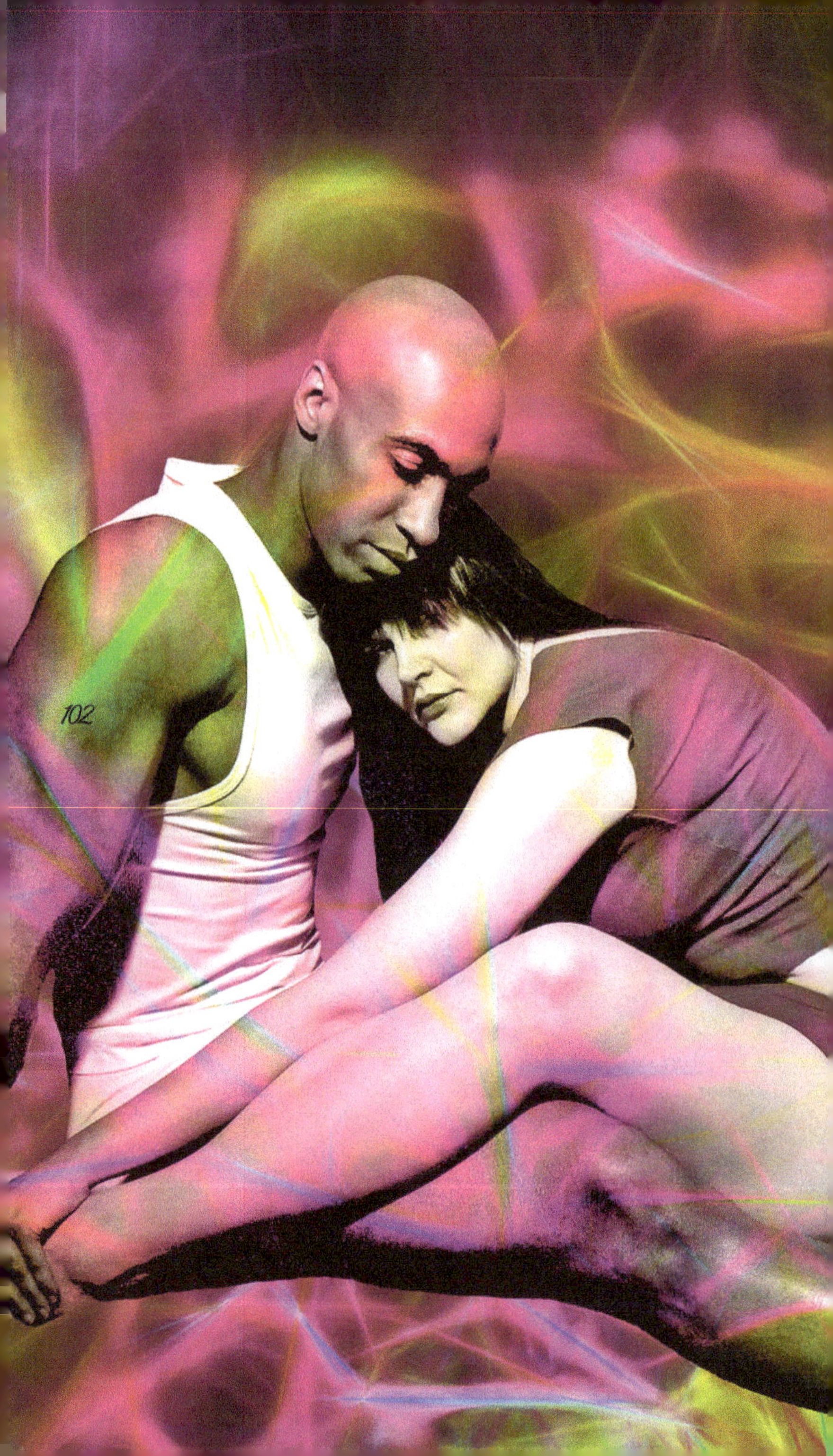

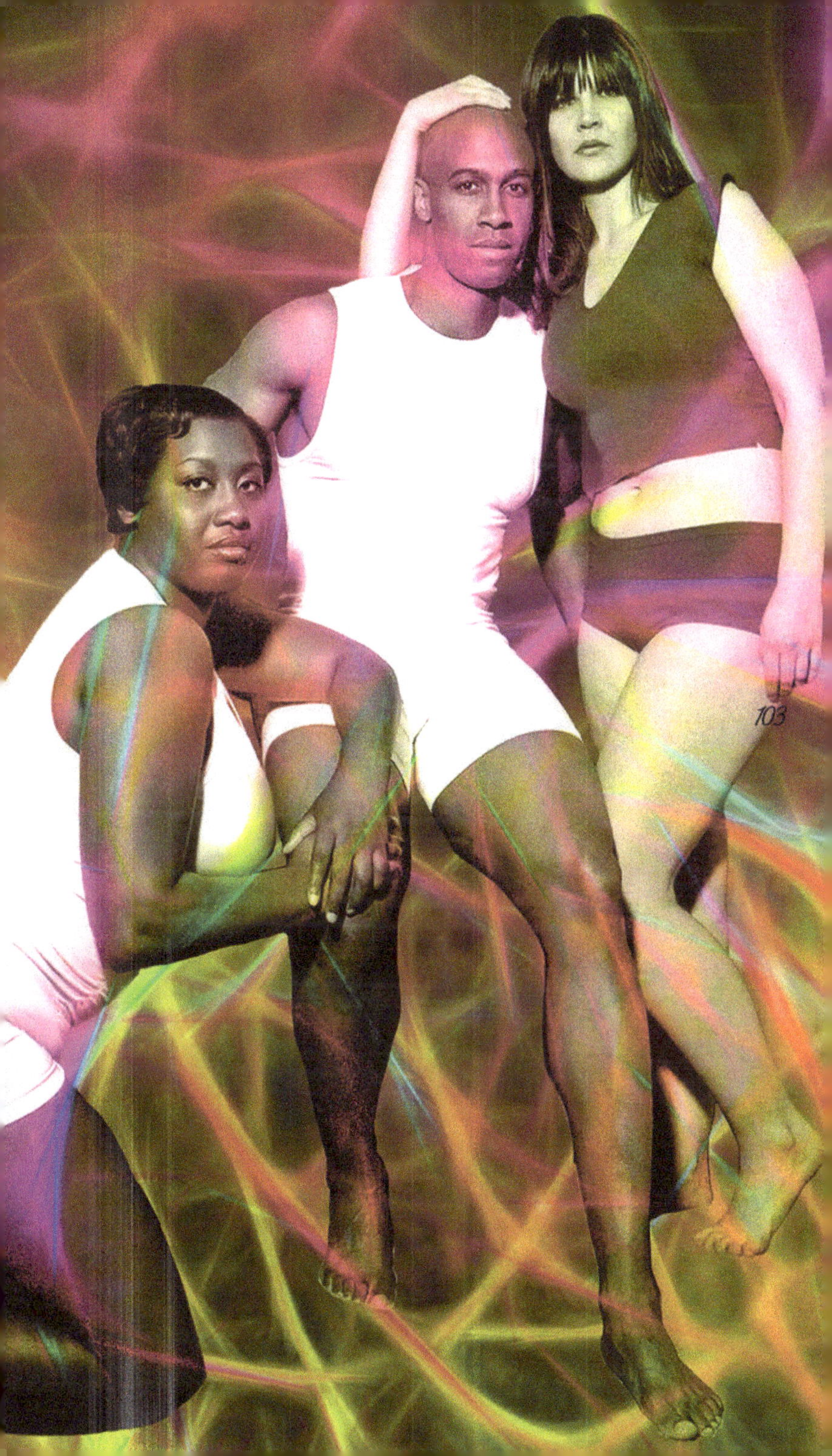

The Moment

Stars resided in my eyes
My heart fluttered and ached
My body trembled with
Just the thought of your approach
I was in my own
Insulated heaven until
The moment you spoke

All was right with me
My world showed much promise
Hopes seemed attainable
Everyone else saw the impossibility
For various reasons
I now recognize the
Insanity of my obsession
From that moment you spoke

So condescending
So arrogant and discourteous
With no reason to be so rude
For all I offered –
Open admiration and devotion –
Any other man would graciously accept

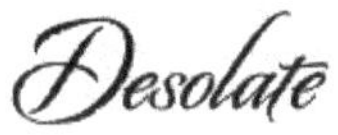

my soul is weeping
flooded with pain
hope all gone

spent two and a half days
with my awakener
searching for a spark of sunshine
not interested enough to
fabricate a flame
sparked by sexual tension
interesting discovery –
my body didn't ignite
and burn at his proximity
four years ago, he consumed
me, crowded my senses
spurned me

once he was my intoxicant,
dream lover
this weekend he was
just a friend helping
with a project
so I accept it –
no more yearnings for his kiss
then today I saw the one at
the gym and talked to the other
no disjointed thoughts
through the suspended fantasy
I stayed grounded
heart didn't soar
excitement didn't come
amazing

all I want is beauty,
laughter, love, joy in life
perhaps the moment has
passed for these three
head hanging
heart cold
I went home alone
for yet another lonely night
the drive crushed me
realization came:
the fantasies were
my hope, my peace
without an erotic focus
I am desolate

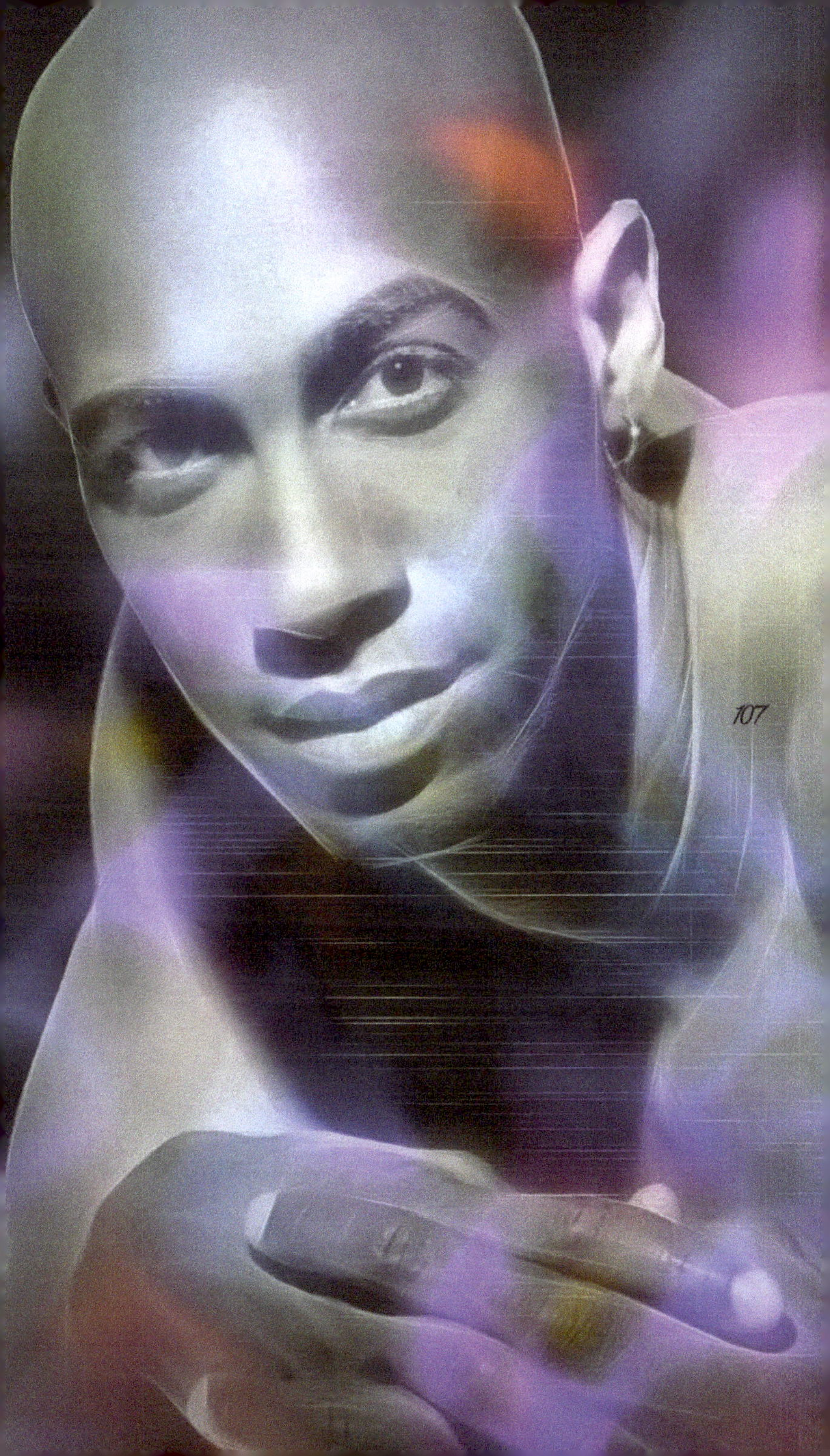

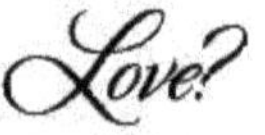

I believe in pure love
Untainted love
Love without physical intimacy
Love for your God
For your parents
Love for your children
But outside of that
What is love to me?
Love is an illusion
A false dependence
Broken promises
And ongoing pain
Love is an ideal
Impossible to capture
To define definitively
To practice completely
Love should be
Reciprocal
But it has only given
Me bitterness
Disillusionment
Endless unfulfilled hopes
A sense of inferiority
And unworthiness
A great awning gap
Of emptiness in my soul
For the mate
Who has yet to come
I have given it
My innocence, my dreams
My freshness, my youth
My idealism.
And greedy Love, took it all.

L'Amour?

Croire dans l'amour pur
L'amour sans souillures
L'amour sans l'intimité charnelle
L'amour pour ton Dieu
Pour tes parents
L'amour pour tes enfants
Mais en dehors de ça
Qu'est-ce que l'amour pour moi?
L'amour est une illusion
Une fausse dépendance
Promesses rompues
Et constante douleur
L'amour est un idéal
Impossible à saisir
À cerner définitivement
À l'exercer complètement
L'amour devrait être
Réciproque
Mais il m'a seulement donné
Amertume
Désenchantement
Espoirs jamais réalisés
Un sentiment d'infériorité
Et d'indignité.
Un vaste abîme béant
Dans mon âme.
Pour le compagnon
Qui doit encore venir
Je lui ai donné
Mon innocence, mes rêves
Ma fraîcheur, ma jeunesse
Mon idéalisme
Et l'amour avide a tout pris.

Superpower

He thinks his superpower
is his handsomeness
Beautiful though he is,
his gentleness was my kryptonite
Until his cavalier dismissiveness
left callouses on my heart

He was a super man
when his strength represented
shelter for my vulnerability
I would've given anything to explore
the known and unknown in his arms
Holding him as he held me
I would've sacrificed
my selfishness to be his
fortress of solitude
Nurturing him even as he fed me

Though I prayed for a man
who stands strong in his power,
I truly need one
who revels in wielding his gentleness
Everything I've asked for in a partner,
I've worked to match
Love is my fortifying mantle,
compassion my laser focus

His short-sightedness
didn't allow for any hope of us
My disappointment paved the way
to my own origin story:
she who sought love from another
found it within herself

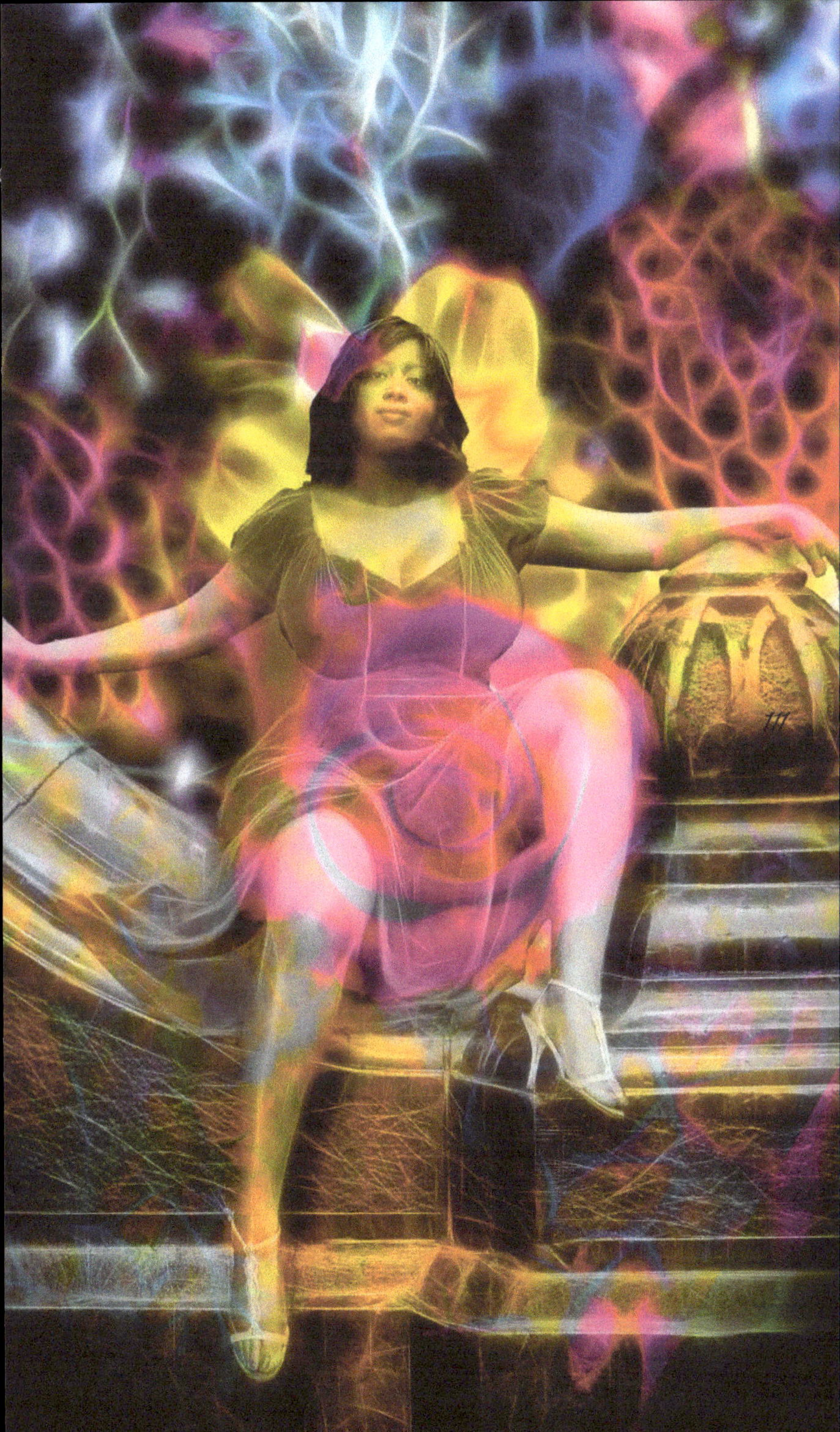

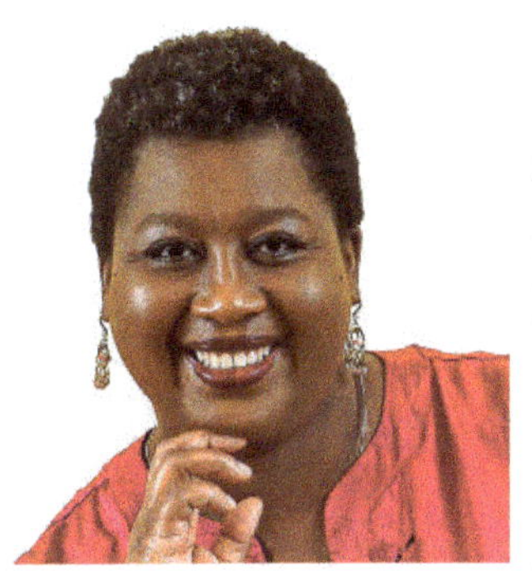

LaShawnda Jones is an independent author, photographer and publisher for Harvest Life. Her work focuses on women, spiritual growth, and social justice.

LaShawnda has published several books exploring the impact of childhood sexual trauma in adulthood as well as the challenges and joys of applying principles of faith in all her interactions.

She holds an interdisciplinary degree in Political Science and French as well as a M.A. in International Affairs. She has studied in France and Poland with missionary training in New York City and Israel. As a member of the RAINN Speaker's Bureau and the Black Speakers Collection, LaShawnda is available for speaking engagements nationally. She is also available for photography assignments. Her body of work can be viewed on **Harvest-Life.org.**

Harvest Life Publishing

Books by
LaShawnda Jones

Spiritual Growth

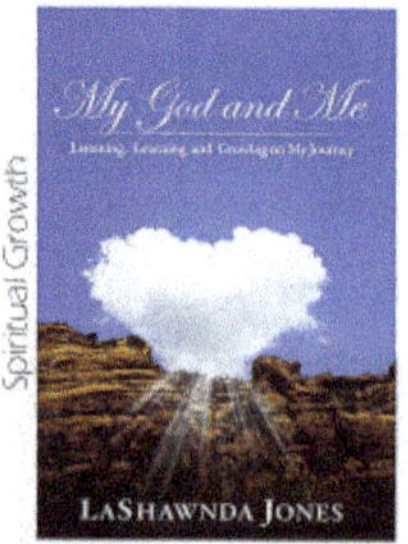

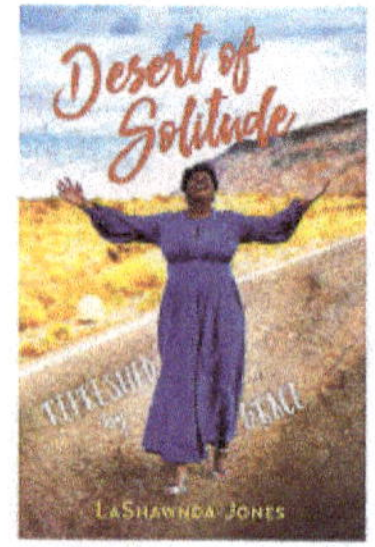

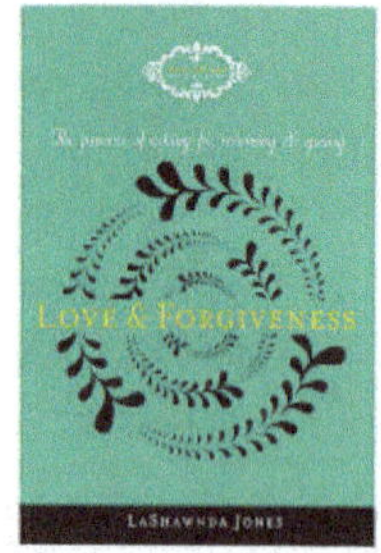

Poetry

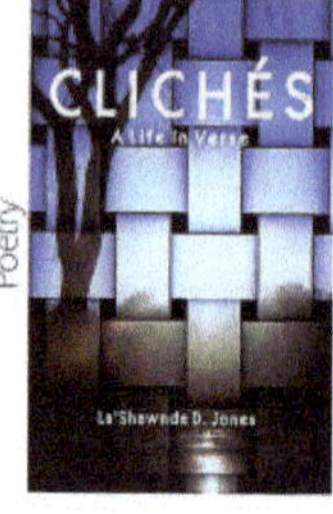

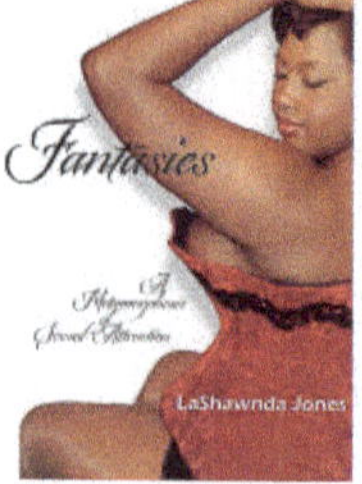

Photography
African American Women

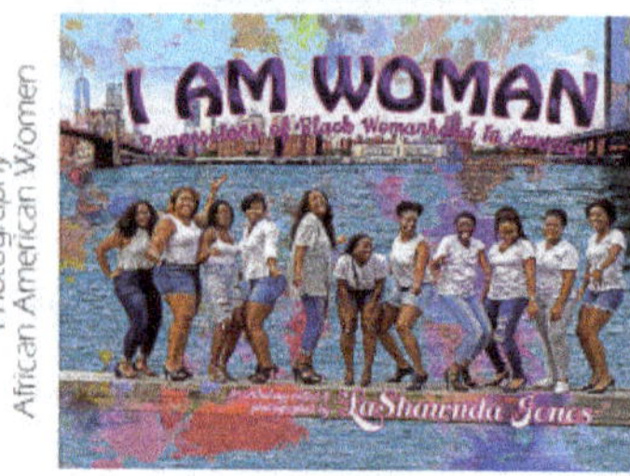

Reachable via:

Blog: Harvest-Life.org/blog
Email: Shawnda @harvest-Life.org
Web3: HarvestLife.eth

@HarvestLifer
on Anchor, Fanbase,
Instagram, Opensea,
Patreon, Twitter

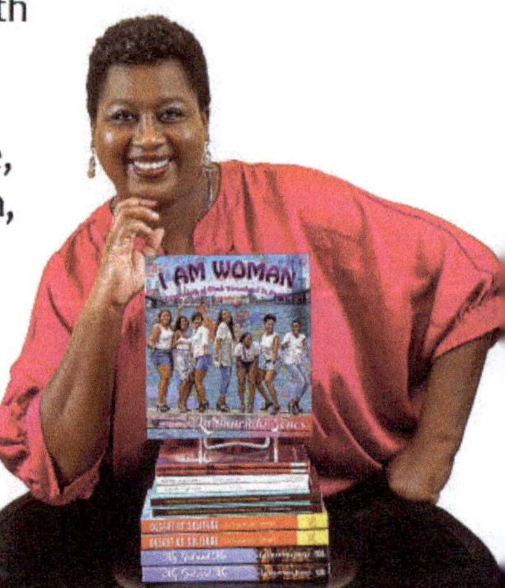

CREDITS

Photographers	Lisa Richelle, *Project Photographer* *pp. 18, 28, 38, 39, 58, 60, 68, 74, 81, 92, 102, 103, 107* Shalina Ali, *pp. Cover, 1, 8, 12, 30, 48, 69, 78* Jason Lam, *pp. 53, 111* Quiana Reed, *p. 65* Willis Roberts, *p. 86*
Models	Philip Griffin LaShawnda Jones Jennifer Olsen
Photo Editors	John Polito (2005) LaShawnda Jones (2021)
Cover Design	LaShawnda Jones
Copy Editor	Olena Jennings
Translators	Barbara J. Collignon (Round 1) Jean Louis Rameaux (Round 2)

www.ingramcontent.com/pod-product-compliance
Ingram Content Group UK Ltd.
Pitfield, Milton Keynes, MK11 3LW, UK
UKHW021835270726
14058UKWH00002B/171

9 780977 617968